A World of Movies

A WORLD OF
MOVIES
70 Years of Film History

by Richard Lawton

with captions by Hugo Leckey

and an introduction by Ella Smith

Delacorte Press — New York

Published by
Delacorte Press, New York

An original work produced by
Vineyard Books, Inc.
159 East 64th Street
New York, N.Y. 10021

Dell TM 681510. Dell Publishing Co., Inc.

Printed in Italy by Arnoldo Mondadori Editore, Sp A

for

John E. Allen

Contents

Introduction   9

The Silents   23

The Talkies   101

Academy Awards   371

Index   377

Acknowledgments   383

May Irwin and John C. Rice in *The Kiss*, 1896

Introduction

by Ella Smith

In 1896, Georges Méliès stopped his camera while filming *The Vanishing Lady*—and the lady skipped out. He continued to shoot, producing a startling effect: when the film was shown, there was suddenly no lady.

Méliès had learned how to do this by accident. He was filming traffic on a Paris street one day when his camera jammed. He fixed it and went on shooting. The image he was recording when he stopped was replaced by another when he continued—and the printed footage showed a bus turn into a hearse. Stop motion—one of the principal components of trick photography—had been born.

Experimentation with the movie camera was present in several countries by 1896. It ranged from the reporting of news (sometimes real, sometimes faked) to the *May Irwin-John C. Rice Kiss* (a 15-second two-shot of a scene from the play *The Widow Jones* which prompted demands for censorship).

But Georges Méliès, French magician and theatre owner, went beyond reporting or recording. He used film to tell a story. In addition, he developed many of the optical tricks used in movie making: double exposure, animation, dissolves, fast and slow motion. Combining these with his theatrical background, he crammed nearly 500 films with spectacle and illusion. He never tired (although his audience must have) of the effects he could create. Ghosts materialized, jugglers lost props in midair and actors changed sex at will.

For all of his inventiveness, however, Méliès was limited in his approach to film making. His camera recorded from only one position: front row center. Actors moved as they would on a stage, and there was no cutting within scenes. His stories were theatrically—not cinematically—told.

Edwin S. Porter—filming for the Edison Company in America—was influenced by Méliès (and possibly by the British) and, in 1903, achieved cinematic narration through his editing of *The Life of an American Fireman*. By arranging time and space to suit his purpose (showing one locale, cutting to another, cutting back to the first) he was working with film on its own terms.

In *The Great Train Robbery* he gave the country its first Western—the blueprint for many that would follow. Made in New Jersey, the film moved swiftly and provided audiences with good guys, bad guys, gun battles and a chase. Broncho Billy Anderson, playing a bit role, went on to become the first cowboy star—making nearly 400 one-reel Westerns in California.

"Moving pictures" in America were at first shown in penny arcades. (A penny dropped into the slot of a machine called the Kinetoscope allowed the viewer to turn a crank and watch a subject in motion.) When screen projection became possible, they were shown in vaudeville houses. Finally they were transferred to the nickelodeon: a converted store with screen, projector and chairs. By 1908 there were eight to ten thousand of these—but they were stuffy, ill-smelling places frequented by the poor and illiterate, and they would not improve until their product was good enough to attract a different audience.

Into this scene came a man who would bring order out of chaos. Within seven years, David Wark Griffith would master the art of the silent film—and the motion picture industry would flourish.

Griffith began his film career with reluctance. A playwright and actor from the legitimate theatre, he was working at New York's Biograph Studio out of necessity. (Theatre people considered movies "galloping tintypes"—a form of entertainment not likely to distinguish itself.) His first directorial effort, *The Adventures of Dollie*, followed the pattern set by Porter but was more successful. It led to a contract with Biograph at $100 a week.

Griffith soon became interested in his work. He abandoned existing formulas and invented new ones. His cameraman, Billy Bitzer, would protest that something couldn't be done—and Griffith would answer "That's why we'll do it." In this manner, he advanced pictures from novelty to art form.

He photographed a scene from more than one setup. He brought the camera closer to his players (resulting in "half an actor"—disturbing to the front office, but accepted by the public). He timed shots for psychological effect. He focused on objects—or portions of players, such as their hands—to point up ideas. And he introduced a more natural acting style to fit the intimacy of the medium. Lillian Gish, in a recent interview, said Griffith "taught that you must not be caught acting. The audience won't believe you if they catch you acting. You must *be* whatever [the character] is."

Differences of opinion with the front office made Griffith leave Biograph in 1913 and, taking Bitzer and many of his actors with him, he became head of production for the Mutual Film Corporation. The setup, at $1000 a week, guaranteed him the right to make two pictures of his own each year in exchange for the "potboilers" he was to turn out for the company.

1915 saw the full effect of Griffith's genius when the 12-reel *Birth of a Nation* was released. Its dramatization of the Civil War and Reconstruction aroused audiences and provoked controversy. Woodrow Wilson said it was "like writing history with lightning"—and the full potential of the motion picture was revealed in that statement. No matter what a film maker wished to say, he had at his disposal a powerful medium if he could learn how to handle it.

One of Griffith's most important contributions (the intercutting of parallel action) reached its peak in his other masterpiece, *Intolerance*. Here, working with four separate plots unfolding simultaneously, he gradually shortened the time given to each. By cutting with increasing rapidity, he was able to build to a climax of epic proportions.

The Birth of a Nation was a box-office hit. *Intolerance*—too complex for 1916 audiences—was not. In fact, Griffith spent years paying off the debts of the latter. But the impact of both films on the future of the industry probably has no equal.

What Griffith was to drama, Mack Sennett was to comedy. Sennett had joined Biograph in 1908 as an actor and, learning from Griffith, had gone on to direct. By 1912, his Keystone Studio on the coast was turning out a unique brand of slapstick. Hundreds of two-reelers presented the gag, the chase and—above all—the impossible. Pies, punches and policemen flew through the air. Clowns such as Ford Sterling, Mabel Normand, Fatty Arbuckle, Chester Conklin and Ben Turpin kept things spinning—and Sennett's editing was a show in itself. The four greatest comedians the screen has known—Charles Chaplin, Buster Keaton, Harold Lloyd and Harry Langdon—trained with Sennett. So did many top directors, such as Frank Capra—whose experience as a gag man at Keystone would result in endless fun in his films (as well as the best direction Langdon ever had).

Southern California—whose favorable climate had been attracting moviemakers since 1910—was soon leading the world in film production. By 1915, the big names were in charge: Goldwyn, Lasky, Zukor, Ince, Fox. Men of extraordinary foresight, they would shape the industry through their ability to sense what the public wanted and to package this profitably.

Goldwyn and Lasky started in Hollywood as partners, producing—for their first feature—Cecil B. DeMille's *The Squaw Man*. Lasky later merged with Zukor (into what would become Paramount Pictures) and Goldwyn founded his own company. Zukor had been one of the first to realize movies could be more than 5¢ one-reelers in nickelodeons. When Griffith made the two-reel *Enoch Arden* in 1911, Biograph released it in two installments. Demands from the public that it be shown in only one influenced others. In 1912, Zukor imported the French *Queen Elizabeth*—a four-reel film starring Sarah Bernhardt—and charged $1.00 admission to the fashionable audience that viewed it in New York's Lyceum Theatre. From here he developed his concept of "Famous Players in Famous Plays"—modifying this when the screen's requirements proved different from those of the stage.

Ince, famous for the many Westerns he turned out starring William S. Hart, formulated the system for making pictures that would be in use three decades later: a detailed scenario, an ironclad shooting schedule, and tight producer control. And Fox made his mark (and his first million) when he took the unknown Theodosia Goodman and groomed her for stardom—resulting in the screen's first vamp: Theda Bara.

Stars would become the major attraction at the box office. Initially, players had been unidentified. As the public acquired favorites, it supplied them with names. Some were taken from the characters portrayed: Little Mary for Mary Pickford, Broncho Billy for G.M. Anderson. Others came from the name of the performer's studio: the Biograph girl, the Imp girl, the Vitagraph girl.

Carl Laemmle changed all this in 1910 when he lured Florence Lawrence, the popular Biograph girl, from her studio by raising her salary and featuring her name. Subsequent publicity guaranteed attendance at her films, a higher rental for them—and power in the hands of the stars.

The earliest stars—such as Lillian and Dorothy Gish, Constance and Norma Talmadge, Clara Kimball Young, Mae Marsh, Mary Pickford, John Bunny, Maurice Costello, Flora Finch and Blanche Sweet—were thus chosen by the public. Attempts to create others, by bringing prominent stage stars to the screen, worked only with those who could adapt to the medium and capture the public's interest.

For stars who clicked, the rewards were great. Two of the most successful of all time, Charles Chaplin and Mary Pickford, are classic examples. Chaplin rose from $150 a week at Keystone in 1913 to over a million dollars for eighteen months' work in 1917. Mary Pickford went from $25 a week at Biograph in 1909 to the same million dollar bracket in 1917. (It took her longer, but she started before salaries were large or stars were stars. Actually, by 1913—when Chaplin was making $150 at Keystone—Pickford was making $500 at Famous Players.)

Also earning a million a year by 1917 was Douglas Fairbanks. These three artists—Chaplin with his Little Tramp, Pickford as America's Sweetheart and Fairbanks with acrobatics and optimism—captured the public's heart. Audiences identified with Chaplin's Little Fellow, they fell in love with Little Mary's vitality and they warmed to Fairbanks' exuberance and marveled at his prowess with stunts. Such performers could write their own ticket—and did. Financially shrewd and capable of running things themselves, they founded the United Artists Corporation in 1919—in partnership with D.W. Griffith—to produce and distribute their own pictures.

Second only to the "big three" in 1917 was William S. Hart, the first of the great Western stars. Ince's top attraction, Hart had been brought up on the frontier, and shaped his character—the Good Bad Man—from past experience. His was the forerunner of the adult Western—authentic, unglamourous and tough. But in that same year, Tom Mix began scoring at Fox with an entirely different kind of cowboy—and would eventually outstrip his predecessor. (Mix injected energy that the aging Hart—who had begun his film career late—no longer had, and substituted showmanship for realism. By 1920, Mix was in the lead. Both men, however, exerted lasting influence on the Western.)

From 1916 to 1925, Hollywood dominated the film market. World War I had forced many European countries to curtail production. Germany, under government subsidy, flourished—making contributions that would have lasting influence, especially on the art film. Sweden and Denmark were also active. But, throughout the years of the conflict, most of the world's "escape" was provided by Hollywood.

The world's first film studio, 1893

During this time, major changes took place in the States. Movies became a "respectable" form of entertainment, and the middle class eagerly sought illusion. Neighborhood theatres sprang up, edging the nickelodeons out. In 1914, opulence took over when the Strand Theatre opened on Broadway with crystal chandeliers, thick carpets and rich ornamentation. Its 3300 seats, 30-piece symphony orchestra and sumptuous lounges delighted patrons, and inspired the building of plush movie houses throughout the country. ("Motion picture cathedrals" reached their height with the Roxy in 1927 and Radio City Music Hall in 1932—both seating over 6000. $150,000 a week was not uncommon at the box office.)

Public taste dictated what Hollywood filmed—as it always would. When something caught on, it was repeated—ad nauseum. Thus, while certain types of movies were staples (Westerns always made money) others were fads that expired when the public had had enough.

For a brief period the war film was popular, but those in the vaults when the war ended were liabilities to the companies that owned them. An exception was Charles Chaplin's *Shoulder Arms,* released shortly before the armistice. Its use of comic fantasy to present the horrors of war (Chaplin is an army private who suffers through training camp but, in a dream, wins the war singlehanded) proved highly successful with audiences tired of propaganda and scare tactics. (The great realistic war pictures—such as King Vidor's *The Big Parade* and William Wellman's *Wings*—would come later, inspired by firsthand experience on the part of the writers or directors involved with them.)

In the game of anticipating public taste, none was shrewder than producer-director Cecil B. DeMille. From the start, he had worked with one eye on the box office. When his first film—a Western—did well, he quickly made several more.

Following the war, DeMille sensed that audiences were tired of stereotyped heroes, heroines, villains and vamps. Victorianism was giving way to the Jazz Age. Sex and luxury—in a country that was discovering the first, and had been deprived of the second—would be more likely to appeal.

DeMille made his contribution to the New Morality by breaking with Puritan tradition. He introduced human fallibility and extravagance. His depiction of bath and boudoir raised the standard of living for some—and of longing for others. And his sociological dissection of marriage was a first. In such films as *Don't Change Your Husband* and *Why Change Your Wife?* he showed that husbands and wives did not always live happily ever after as had been supposed. Often they indulged in infidelity. They were always driven to it, of course. Even DeMille wasn't that modern. And virtue did triumph. But not until the audience had had its fill of vice.

DeMille's star attraction in these romps was Gloria Swanson, who became his "emancipated woman." Swanson's initial training had been with Mack Sennett, and she knew how to get laughs. Yet she was a skilled dramatic actress. In addition, she projected glamour. Satins, jewels, furs—and brilliantined coiffures—became her. Through her handling of humor and *haute couture*—and her fiery

The Great Train Robbery, 1903

spirit—she made the emancipated woman something to reckon with.

If the American woman was getting out of hand, it would take a different approach from the American male to tame her. Rudolph Valentino—most popular romantic idol of all time—provided it. (In fact, he and Swanson were later teamed in Elinor Glyn's *Beyond the Rocks* in order to capitalize on this.) An actor in minor roles or films for over five years, Valentino had attracted little attention in Hollywood until suddenly a hunch was played. He was cast as a Latin lover in *The Four Horsemen of the Apocalypse*. Women succumbed, and his future was assured. *The Sheik* set a new style in screen love-making. (So profound—and unhealthy—an effect did Valentino have on his public that his premature death in 1926 produced world-wide hysteria and a number of suicides.)

Passion and loose living on the screen (originally restricted to villains and vamps who paid for their "sinful ways") appeared to be headed for trouble when scandal *behind* the cameras brought cries of protest from moralists. The murder of director William Desmond Taylor, the accidental death of actress Virginia Rappe after a drinking party given by Fatty Arbuckle—and the death of actor Wallace Reid from drugs—led to the importation of Will Hays (former postmaster general and future Hollywood figurehead) to clean things up at a salary of $100,000 a year. "Morality clauses" were inserted in contracts, and the industry took on internal censorship in order to avoid external. Efforts were made to placate the public. Chief placator was Cecil B. DeMille with *The Ten Commandments*. But, after the storm had blown over, internal censorship slackened—and audiences were soon watching Colleen Moore in *Flaming Youth*, DeMille's *The Golden Bed* and Clara Bow in *It*.

While it may not sound like it, high living was only a small portion of what appeared on the screen in the twenties. Not everyone wanted to be liberated. Mary Pickford continued to please with *Little Annie Rooney*, *Sparrows* and *My Best Girl*. Douglas Fairbanks was a hit with swashbuckling romances in exotic settings. And Lillian Gish was top box office in Griffith's *Broken Blossoms*, *Way Down East* and *Orphans of the Storm*. In addition, important strides were being made in some of the genres.

The Western acquired a new stature when James Cruze filmed *The Covered Wagon* in 1923. His re-creation of pioneer hardships against vast panoramic settings showed what epic treatment could achieve. Soon every aspect of the West's expansion was being explored. In *The Iron Horse* John Ford dealt with the construction of the transcontinental railroad. The pony express, the Indian wars and the Oklahoma land rush—all became material for the big-scale Western, one of America's classic contributions to the screen.

Another American strength—comedy—reached a peak in the twenties. Unlike the Western, whose action would be enhanced by the coming of sound, pantomimic comedy would suffer. But as long as films were silent, the universal language of Chaplin, Keaton, Lloyd and Langdon spoke to everybody.

All four of these comedians started with Mack Sennett and then struck out on their own. Each perfected characters who survived in the harsh cruel world through a particular specialty. Chaplin used his wits, Keaton rode things out, Lloyd moved fast and Langdon trusted.

Chaplin was the most complex. An indomitable spirit who shrugged off defeat—yet one who felt it keenly. Like all great clowns, he could break your heart.

Keaton was a study in determination. Sad-eyed, vulnerable—but capable of superhuman achievement.

Lloyd was well-adjusted. Eager to please, quick, all smiles. A Horatio Alger sure he would win.

And Langdon was the innocent child. Unable to help himself. Generally unaware even that he needed help.

The first three comedians were self-sufficient. Chaplin wrote and directed his own material; Keaton and Lloyd used gag men and directors, but were also in control. Langdon who—unlike the others—had not created his character and did not fully understand him, was brilliantly directed in his first three features by Frank Capra. But Langdon wanted to take over too. When he did, he wrecked his career.

Outstanding at this time too was Lon Chaney, whose first grotesque was the crippled beggar in *The Miracle Man*. Also self-sufficient, Chaney specialized in the deformed and the demented. He created elaborate make-up, bound his body into contortion and executed stunts that aggravated the pain. In *The Penalty* he was a legless man, in *The Unknown*—armless, in *West of Zanzibar*—a paralytic. One of his greatest portrayals remains Quasimodo in the 1923 *Hunchback of Notre Dame*. A master of mime and pathos, Chaney made a contribution to the silents that was unique.

Strongly influential in the twenties were European film makers—especially the Germans. When New York audiences went wild over Pola Negri in Ernst Lubitsch's *Passion* (the American title for *Madame Dubarry*) both actress and director were invited to make films in America. Subsequent successes brought other artists to the States. From Sweden: Victor Seastrom who would direct Lillian Gish in *The Scarlet Letter* and *The Wind;* Mauritz Stiller who brought his protégé, Greta Garbo, with him. From Germany: E.A. Dupont who had written and directed *Variety;* F.W. Murnau who had directed *The Last Laugh* and Paul Leni who would show promise with *The Cat and the Canary*—until both their careers were cut short by untimely death; Josef von Sternberg whose textures, shadows and exotic portraits of Marlene Dietrich would make him the greatest creator of visual poetry the American screen has known.

What had caught Hollywood's eye in the German films was not so much what they were saying (although this would have its effect too) but how they were saying it: with the subjective camera—as in *The Last Laugh* and *Variety* where the camera moves as if it were the actor, seeing from his point of view; with expressionist techniques—as in *The Cabinet of Dr. Caligari* where painted perspective and bizarre make-up and gestures show the world of a madman; with low-key lighting, slower tempos and unusual camera angles.

This technical progress was soon assimilated by Hollywood—and motion pictures began benefiting from the exposure of European and American craftsmen to each other. The German director to make the most significant contribution under this arrangement was F.W. Murnau whose poetic and moving *Sunrise* remains a classic. The American director to score most highly under the same circumstances was King Vidor whose realistic and equally moving *The Crowd* is another. Both pictures are prime examples of the maturity that had been reached by 1928 in the art of film making.

Silents were invariably accompanied by music. Many—such as *The Birth of a Nation*—had elaborate symphonic scores for the orchestras of the first-run houses, and simplified versions for the pianos of the smaller ones. In 1926, Warners' introduction of the Vitaphone—a sound on disc process which added a synchronized musical score to *Don Juan*—foreshadowed the end of live accompaniment and of the silent film. In 1927, Al Jolson sang and spoke briefly in *The Jazz Singer* and—by 1928—Warners had turned out the first feature-length all-talkie: *The Lights of New York.*

The conversion to sound was swift. Spurred by the success of *The Jazz Singer*, major studios raced to acquire sound systems and push talkies into production. Silents already in progress became part-talkies through the insertion of a reel or two of dialogue. The last important picture to be done as a silent (by a studio wanting to capitalize on its prize star for as long as possible) was M-G-M's *The Kiss*—and Greta Garbo did draw audiences. But even Garbo would have to talk in her next film if she was to survive. (Unlike so many stars whose careers ended when they spoke, Garbo not only survived, she triumphed—when *Anna Christie* revealed a voice as sultry as her image.) The one star to cling to silents and get away with it was Charles Chaplin whose 1931 *City Lights* and 1936 *Modern Times* (except for a song and a few lines) contained only music and sound effects.

For a while studios turned out both talking and silent versions of their pictures, in order to accommodate theatres not yet wired for sound. But by 1929, when nearly half the nation's houses had switched over, this was no longer necessary. Silents were a thing of the past—and increased box-office attendance left no doubt about the public's enthusiasm for talkies.

Initially, talkies were a novelty for the public—and a headache for the industry. First there was the problem of *how* to film. The ease and fluidity with which the camera had been moving was halted by the need to plan business

14

Florence Lawrence, 1911

around a stationary mike, and by the fact that the camera and its operator were now enclosed in a soundproof booth. (In time, booms would allow mikes to follow players, and cameras would be equipped with noiseless gears.)

Then there was the problem of *what* to film. Exploitation of sound made many forget that the primary responsibility of movies is to move. The importation of Broadway plays and actors (the latter because they could talk) resulted in an abundance of "canned theatre": static presentations of scripts that were heavy on dialogue and light on action.

Musicals offered greater possibilities for movement and did better. Warners made the first two-color Technicolor musical feature, *On With the Show,* in 1929. Hit musicals of that year included *The Gold Diggers of Broadway, Sunny Side Up* with Janet Gaynor and Charles Farrell and the Academy Award-winning *Broadway Melody.* The operetta was introduced with John Boles in *The Desert Song.* "All-star revues" (Warners' *Show of Shows,* M-G-M's *Hollywood Revue, Paramount on Parade,* the *Fox Movietone Follies* and Universal's *King of Jazz*) featured—in some sort of routine—just about every performer on the studio rosters.

The drawing power of the early musical was short-lived, however—partly because there were so many, and partly because their staging lacked imagination. By 1931 only Eddie Cantor's were good box office. This was due mainly to Cantor's popularity, but it should also be noted that his dance director—Busby Berkeley—was a contributing factor. Berkeley, who had been imported from the Broadway stage by Samuel Goldwyn, immediately saw that movie and stage choreography should not be the same. In his work on the Cantor musicals, he explored the camera's potential for creating illusion. While the results cannot be compared to what he would achieve later at Warners, they do have style and authority.

Like Berkeley, others with vision were experimenting with ways of getting talkies on their feet. Four directors already in the industry (King Vidor, Lewis Milestone, Ernst Lubitsch and Josef von Sternberg) and a newcomer who had directed on the New York stage (Rouben Mamoulian) achieved superior blends of sound and silence which set courses for others.

Basically, what these men did was to minimize dialogue, select sounds that would be dramatically effective, and liberate the camera by shooting some of their scenes silently and adding sound tracks later. Vidor's *Hallelujah* showed a chase through swamps against an impressionistic sound track with larger-than-life amplification. Milestone's *All Quiet on the Western Front* balanced carefully-scored battle noises with tracking shots. Lubitsch's *The Love Parade* joined dialogue and song into the first cinematic musical. Von Sternberg's *Morocco* combined silence and beating drums with a smouldering visual. And Mamoulian's *Applause*—in addition to being a remarkable first film—used two mikes and two channels recording simultaneously.

From the studios themselves came other firsts. One was the gangster film—an outgrowth of Warners' decision to film topical material that would have meaning for depression audiences. Prominent in the headlines of the day were those who lived outside the law. In 1930, Mervyn LeRoy's *Little Caesar* showed the rise and fall of the first of these: Edward G. Robinson's Caesar Enrico Bandello. A cynical and hard-hitting approach reflected the unrest of the era, and set a precedent for some sixty underworld films that would follow—the most outstanding being William Wellman's *The Public Enemy* with James Cagney and Howard Hawks' *Scarface* with Paul Muni. Taut dialogue, swift editing and car chases with machine guns and squealing tires showed that movies had found a way to move again—both literally and with the times.

Depression films showed women living outside the law too. Poverty and disillusionment or—simply—attraction to money, made rich men's mistresses out of Barbara Stanwyck, Joan Crawford, Greta Garbo and Marlene Dietrich in *Baby Face, Possessed, Susan Lenox* and *The Blonde Venus.* Unlike the gangster, who was killed for his transgressions, the errant female could repent and reform. But before the gangster "got his" or the fallen woman "went straight" they had a pretty glamourous time of it. Violence and sex looked extremely rewarding and—as the depression grew worse and attendance at the box office declined—producers exploited this even more.

Inevitably, pressure groups became concerned. The rate at which heroines were having illegitimate babies was alarming; the popularity of sex symbols Jean Harlow and Clara Bow was even more upsetting; and the last straw was the appearance on the scene of Mae West—whose reason for being a fallen woman was because she liked it, and who didn't know what the words repent or reform meant. Shortly after the release of her second film, in 1933, the National Legion of Decency was formed and the motion picture industry was in for another cleanup.

It emerged with a new Production Code and turned its attention to safer material. Romance and adventure were provided through a focus on earlier days and nobler characters. *Little Women, The Barretts of Wimpole Street, David Copperfield, Mutiny on the Bounty* and *The Adventures of Robin Hood* showed Katharine Hepburn, Norma Shearer, W.C. Fields, Clark Gable and Errol Flynn in favorable lights. *Romeo and Juliet* and *A Midsummer Night's Dream* didn't get anybody into trouble either.

The social scene was not neglected but it was handled differently. Topical influence was slipped into musicals and comedies, which generally disguised it enough to get it by the censors. (In 1935, even the gangster returned: as the G-man—whose tactics were the same as those of the gangster, but who was okay because he was on the side of the law.)

As technical equipment improved, thirties films acquired polish. The fluidity that sound had interrupted was restored, and film makers found they had more to work with than they had had in the silent days. (Certainly no one missed the awkward subtitle.) A wide variety of styles was explored and mastered.

The horror film came of age with Tod Browning's *Dracula* and James Whale's *Frankenstein:* both products of Hollywood's horror factory, Universal, where their stars—Bela Lugosi and Boris Karloff—would have long and prosperous careers. Horror became art in the 1932 *Dr. Jekyll and Mr. Hyde* through the talents of Rouben Mamoulian and Fredric March. And it was turned into spectacle in Cooper and Schoedsack's *King Kong*, with trick photography and a screaming Fay Wray.

The epic Western benefited handsomely. It was now accompanied by sounds as stirring as its themes—and it moved majestically from Wesley Ruggles' 1931 *Cimarron* to the 1939 classics of John Ford and Cecil B. DeMille: *Stagecoach* and *Union Pacific*.

In 1933, the musical enjoyed a renaissance—due partly to the fluidity with which directors had learned to work and partly to two special talents. The first of these—Busby Berkeley—created a sensation at Warners when he staged the dances for Lloyd Bacon's *42nd Street* and *Footlight Parade* and Mervyn LeRoy's *Gold Diggers of 1933*. Now in top form, Berkeley was photographing from every angle—using mirrors, treadmills, kaleidoscopic lenses and matte shots. His overhead camera turned groups of moving chorus girls into flowers and geometric designs. His flamboyant production numbers bore little relationship to the stories in which they appeared but, as cinematic dance spectacles, they had no equal.

The other talent, working at RKO, was Fred Astaire. It was through Astaire that the musical achieved its full sophistication. Astaire choreographed for the camera too—using the facility with which it could cut from one area to another, pull back or pan—but he did not let it intrude. When he and Ginger Rogers floated through their routines in *Roberta* and *Top Hat*, the focus was on dancing. Astaire's approach was functional, and his work joined form and content smoothly.

Comedy—as it had previously existed—was hard hit by sound. The silent comedian had expressed himself solely through action. Those whose characters depended on mime—such as Keaton and Lloyd—were at a loss when dialogue invaded their worlds. (Chaplin's Little Tramp eventually bowed out too.)

A new school of laugh makers took over: The Marx Brothers with wisecracks and nonsense, W.C. Fields with ill temper and eccentricity, Laurel and Hardy and others. Laurel and Hardy were silent comedians who could handle dialogue and, as it happened, did much better in talkies. Fields, also in silents, added the peculiarities of his voice and outlook to his precise pantomime and became a kind of philosopher-comedian. The Marx Brothers were vaudeville imports. The humor of all of these performers was uniquely their own—as was their way of delivering it.

Comedy, as a genre, reached new heights when it had smart dialogue at its disposal. The wit of directors like Ernst Lubitsch—who could give as much class to a word as he could to a look or gesture—produced some of the most polished humor of all time. *Trouble in Paradise*—with Miriam Hopkins and Herbert Marshall as scintillating

swindlers attracted to each other's artistry and bodies, and with an equally sparkling Kay Francis as the rich widow they are trying to rob—is an elegant mixture of trickery and romance. Its eternal triangle is eternal fun.

Hitting between low comedy and high was a genre that incorporated the two. Later tagged screwball comedy, it showed socially acceptable people behaving in socially unacceptable ways. Characters did the unexpected—often in the most outrageous manner possible. In 1934, *It Happened One Night, Twentieth Century* and *The Thin Man* touched off a cycle of screwball comedies that would extend into the forties—replacing the conventions of society with a world people made for themselves.

On the surface, these films were diverting flirtations with irresponsibility. But, beneath this, most of them contained mild attacks on the social scene—or at least some rather unflattering pictures of it. Gregory La Cava's *My Man Godfrey*, Mitchell Leisen's *Easy Living* and Frank Capra's *Mr. Deeds Goes to Town* were all screwball comedies with messages or—as they were also called—social comedies.

Other message pictures dispensed with humor and dealt with the social scene in a grimmer manner. Lynching was the problem presented in Fritz Lang's *Fury*, slums the subject of William Wyler's *Dead End*, migratory workers that of John Ford's 1940 *Grapes of Wrath* and facism that of Anatole Litvak's *Confessions of a Nazi Spy*.

The decade in which moviemakers had wrestled with technological upheaval came to a close—with a bravura exhibition of the success they had achieved. It had taken three years, three directors, five cinematographers and four and a quarter million dollars to bring Margaret Mitchell's epic Civil War novel, *Gone With the Wind*, to the screen. Under the meticulous supervision of producer David O. Selznick, the task was perfectly realized. A splendid cast, a Max Steiner score, and an army of art and special effects people turned this massive undertaking into a three hour and forty minute classic that would be the nation's box-office champion for almost thirty years. Stretched to 70mm in 1968, it was still drawing audiences.

The late thirties had been a lucrative time for the motion picture industry. Spending was high but so were profits. With the outbreak of war in Europe, however, the Continental market was cut off. Other markets shrank and Hollywood's prosperity came to a halt. The studios adopted rigid economy measures—cutting salaries and reducing staffs. 1940 became a year of heavy loss. To make things worse, the government banned block booking: the practice which had forced exhibitors to book a studio's entire yearly output in advance. Now films were to be sold in blocks of five, which theatre owners could view beforehand.

Hollywood met the crisis with better scripts and tighter production methods. 1941 was a year of exceptional pictures: John Ford's *How Green Was My Valley*, Orson Welles' *Citizen Kane*, Frank Capra's *Meet John Doe*, Howard Hawks' *Sergeant York* and *Ball of Fire*, William

Lou Tellegen and Sarah Bernhardt in *Queen Elizabeth*, 1911

Wyler's *The Little Foxes*, John Huston's *The Maltese Falcon* and Preston Sturges' *The Lady Eve*. Needless to say, box-office receipts rose. In 1942, after the U.S. had entered the war, a booming economy and an entertainment-hungry public pushed receipts even higher.

In addition to escapist fare (comedies such as the Crosby and Hope "Road to" films, musicals such as Michael Curtiz' *Yankee Doodle Dandy* and Vincente Minnelli's *Meet Me in St. Louis,* women's pictures such as Irving Rapper's *Now, Voyager*) the war years brought with them a more realistic approach to film making. Newsreels and documentaries contained a surfeit of violence and, inevitably, commercial films did too. Man's inhumanity to man flourished in a genre (later called *film noir*) whose characters were driven by greed, ambition and lust. At its height *film noir* was an unflinching disregard for others—never better shown than in Billy Wilder's classic tale of seduction and murder: *Double Indemnity.*

Film noir had no message. It existed for its own sake. But abnormal behavior was also presented in films whose protagonists were psychotic. In these, the cause was examined. Wilder's *The Lost Weekend*, Alfred Hitchcock's *Spellbound* and Anatole Litvak's *The Snake Pit* made statements about alcoholism, psychoanalysis and mental illness. Perhaps the most significant social statement to come out of the forties, however, was that commissioned by Samuel Goldwyn: William Wyler's *The Best Years of Our Lives.* Dealing with the problem of socio-economic adjustment for those returning to civilian life, it foreshadowed a condition which would engulf the entire country—resulting, for those who could not cope with it, in a world as tortured as that film makers had been creating.

Postwar audiences provided Hollywood with its biggest grosses yet. In 1946 and 1947, weekly film attendance was estimated at 85 million. Within ten years, it would be less than half that figure as a result of another technological advance: television.

Television had been a potential threat since the late thirties. War had halted the new medium's progress by curtailing the manufacture of TV sets and stripping it of its personnel. But when peace and prosperity returned, the inevitable happened. TV developed rapidly and forced the movie industry into a battle for survival—with a competitor whose entertainment was free.

Birth of a Nation, 1915

As profits sank, Hollywood sought ways to draw audiences back to the theatres. The logical answer was to give them something television could not. Three-dimensional and wide-screen processes and stereophonic sound (all invented long ago and shelved for one reason or another) were revived and refined.

In 1952, *This Is Cinerama* made its appearance—using three electronically-synchronized projectors to join images on a wide-angle screen. Its illusion of depth involved audiences in an airplane trip and an unnerving roller coaster ride. Although costly and able to play in only a few specially-equipped theatres, Cinerama survived and improved.

3-D was introduced with Arch Oboler's *Bwana Devil*, a picture best described by the ad for a flat film which asked: Do You Want A Good Movie—Or A Lion In Your Lap? Dependent upon the wearing of Polaroid glasses and the synchronization of two projectors (and far too gimmicky to be taken seriously) 3-D was short-lived. Probably the only film to use it with any taste was Andre de Toth's *House of Wax*.

The process ultimately adopted by the industry in its efforts to outdo television was CinemaScope—launched in 1953 with Henry Koster's *The Robe*. CinemaScope needed no glasses and used only one projector. While it gave little illusion of depth, it did fill a wide screen. An anamorphic lens squeezed an ultra-wide picture onto 35mm film and another lens, attached to the projector, restored the picture to its original width.

The wide screen posed awkward composition problems. It was suitable for the musical, the Western and the historical epic—which is about all it was used for at first—but when intimacy rather than spectacle was required, it was inappropriate. However, with a more sophisticated handling of the camera, wide-screen became the shape of the future.

Hollywood learned not only how to exist with television but also how to benefit from it. A release of pre-1948 films to TV, between 1955 and 1958, brought enormous gains on material that had been gathering dust in vaults. Subsequent movies were equally profitable. In 1966, David Lean's *Bridge on the River Kwai* netted two million dollars for two showings, and leading moviemakers began filming with TV rental in mind. Soon after, TV began fighting high rentals by making movies for theatrical release themselves, in order to compete with Hollywood's. And, ultimately, the rivals have combined forces—as they did in the fifties when TV shows were first shot in film studios—through movies made for television. Despite this latter development, however, movies *not* made for television continue to extract a high rental from it.

Adding to Hollywood's woes in the fifties was a 1948 court decision which ended studio ownership of theatres—and the previously-guaranteed market for volume. In addition to needing better films, the studios now needed fewer. As they cut down on their output, they reduced their overhead by dropping the options of some of their more expensive artists. Directors, writers and stars thus

freed began to work on their own. The result was a move toward personal expression: the development of the independent film maker. United Artists became the backer and distributor for many; new corporations were founded to do the same; and the studios soon had to function in a similar manner (or pay enormous salaries and percentages) to obtain the services of their former top money makers.

Those who produced their own films were able to work with less restraint. They could experiment with controversial subject matter, make their own decisions and film wherever they wanted. (They could also lower their tax rates by taking percentages and benefits instead of salaries.) Yet with greater freedom came greater responsibility. If a film did not show a profit, its creator might never obtain the backing for another. The success of the independent film maker was determined not only by his talent as an artist, but by his executive ability. Thus, director-writer John Huston shot *The African Queen* in ten weeks, under difficult conditions, and came out a winner. Actor Marlon Brando used four years and five million dollars on *One-Eyed Jacks* and failed to meet his costs. Huston continued to produce. Brando did not. (Despite the element of risk involved, however, independent production thrived and would, eventually, take over. Hollywood's efforts to keep the studio system afloat would be defeated—by spiraling costs and changes in the market. The majors would rent their stage space, invest in other businesses and—ultimately—sell out to conglomerates.)

With the rise of independence came the fall of censorship. In the mid-fifties, mature approaches to controversial material, such as Otto Preminger's treatment of prostitution in *The Moon Is Blue* and drug addiction in *The Man with the Golden Arm*, were refused the Production Code's seal of approval. They were released without it and did well. Adult films from Europe were profiting too, not only in the art houses but in some first-run and neighborhood theatres. Films were finally focusing on reality—as literature and the theatre had done long before—and the public was responding.

Envious of the business going to the independents and foreign films, Hollywood decided to liberalize its Code—which was over twenty years old. Alterations were made, but they were so inadequate for the times that they were either loosely interpreted or ignored. As the sixties progressed, the Code was flagrantly disregarded—and finally abandoned. In 1968, voluntary classification took its place.

How well the new freedom has been handled has depended on its reason for being used—on whether it is artistically justified or meant to exploit. The elimination of censorship has unquestionably produced plenty of trash—but, for the most part, it has resulted in honesty rather than sensationalism.

The experimentation which began in the fifties, the influx of foreign films, the end of the studio system and the exchange of ideas and techniques between American and European film makers have had lasting effects. Location shooting—both in the States and abroad—has largely replaced studio process work. Directors and casts from both continents now work together, financed by international arrangements. And movies, as a result, have broadened their outlook.

In America, an increasing concern with the social scene —aided by the fall of censorship—has permeated most of the genres. The historical blockbuster and the musical have changed little—but they have also lost audiences. Stanley Kubrick did add intelligence to the blockbuster in *Spartacus;* but Joseph Mankiewicz—or, more likely, a great many people—subtracted it in *Cleopatra* (at over 40 million dollars, the world's costliest film and probably a reason for the current lack of interest in historical spectacle). Robert Wise knew better than to alter *The Sound of Music,* but this was a one shot—and the cycle of big-budget musicals that followed, hoping to cash in too, did not. Almost without exception, the other genres—drama, science fiction, horror, the gangster film, comedy and the Western—have come to reflect the frustrations of the times.

Bleakest are the science fiction, horror and gangster categories which have discovered, as did Sartre in *No Exit,* that hell is other people. From the "ultra-violence" and moral decay of Kubrick's *Clockwork Orange* to the world of organized crime in Francis Ford Coppola's *The Godfather,* there is no turning back to artificial monsters or vampires. (The supernatural is real now too, and William Friedkin's *The Exorcist* is out to prove it.)

The Western has had a little of everything. It has been burlesqued in Elliot Silverstein's *Cat Ballou* and George Roy Hill's *Butch Cassidy and the Sundance Kid.* It has been given a blood bath in Sam Peckinpah's *The Wild Bunch.* And it has been wrapped in the fragile atmosphere of Robert Altman's *McCabe & Mrs. Miller.*

Contemporary drama has been both perceptive and honest. British director John Schlesinger's misfits in *Midnight Cowboy* and John Avildsen's American businessman in *Save The Tiger* symbolize, respectively, those for whom there is no dream, and those who have abused it. The protagonists of both films operate ruthlessly and without ethics. Material defeat is inevitable in *Cowboy;* spiritual in *Tiger.*

Comedy has not been exempt. Stanley Kubrick's *Dr. Strangelove: or, How I Learned to Stop Worrying and Love the Bomb* is probably the classic "sick comedy"—its picture of those in charge of humanity's fate funny to some, disturbing to all.

Yet, for the most part, laugh makers *are* still producing humor. Screwball comedy was resurrected in Peter Bogdanovich's *What's Up, Doc?.* Romantic comedy is alive and well in Melvin Frank's *A Touch of Class.* And nostalgia has turned Bogdanovich's *Paper Moon* into one of 1973's biggest hits.

Where will it all go from here? It's anybody's guess.

OPPOSITE Theda Bara as *Cleopatra,* 1917

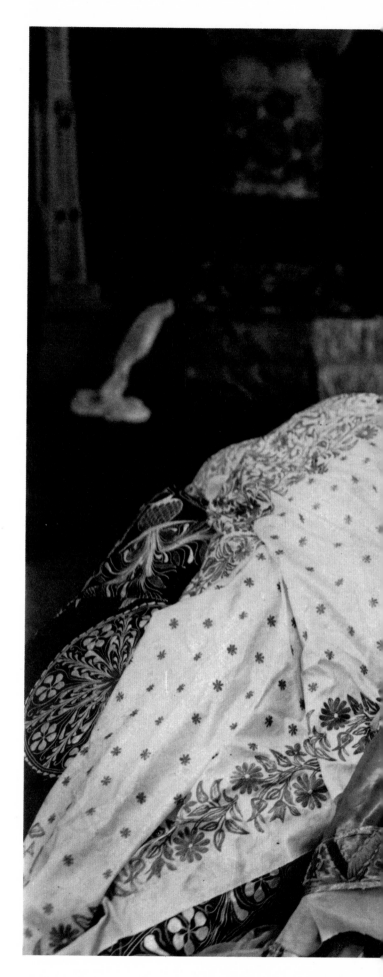

THE SILENTS
The Twenties and Before

ABOVE John Barrymore and Constance Binney in
The Test of Honor, 1919

LEFT Kathryn Adams, 1914

OPPOSITE Marie Doro, 1918

Here is Marie Doro in a publicity shot; she might be the Queen Mother pausing for a glance at the household cavalry. There is a hint of an old master's painting in this picture which was taken when Doro was in her twenties. The costuming and hair style give her a pleasingly mature look, one which is out of favor today when girlishness and fleshy youth are the insisted qualities.

ABOVE Enid Bennet in *The Law of Men*, 1918

RIGHT Bessie Barriscale in *Hater of Men*, 1917

OPPOSITE William S. Hart, 1920

William S. Hart was the greatest cowboy, the archetypal Western hero whose blazing guns and self-assured morality still ring around the globe. It was a vision uncluttered by society, or industrial plague, or women and "gettin' civilized." The cowboy was a loner — except, of course, for his faithful horse who patiently waited for some blushing dalliance with a school marm to peter out. Then off towards the sunset and the once eternal West. Hart rescued the faltering, early Westerns by bringing realism and vitality to them. The film *Pinto Ben* was directed by Hart and based on a poem he had written and dedicated to his horse.

ABOVE Enid Markey in *The Phantom*, 1917

LEFT Thomas Meighan, 1919

OPPOSITE Mae Marsh in *The Wharf Rat*, 1916

The name of Mae Marsh is little known today. Beside more familiar names—the Gish sisters, Valentino, Garbo—hers is rarely mentioned. Nevertheless, film historians call her one of the finest actresses on the silent screen; indeed they rank her as one of the greatest screen actresses of all time. She introduced an understated quality of intense realism to her work in which her anxious hands were a trademark. Throughout her career her best work was achieved under the direction of D.W. Griffith, and her best performance was in his magnificent film *Intolerance*.

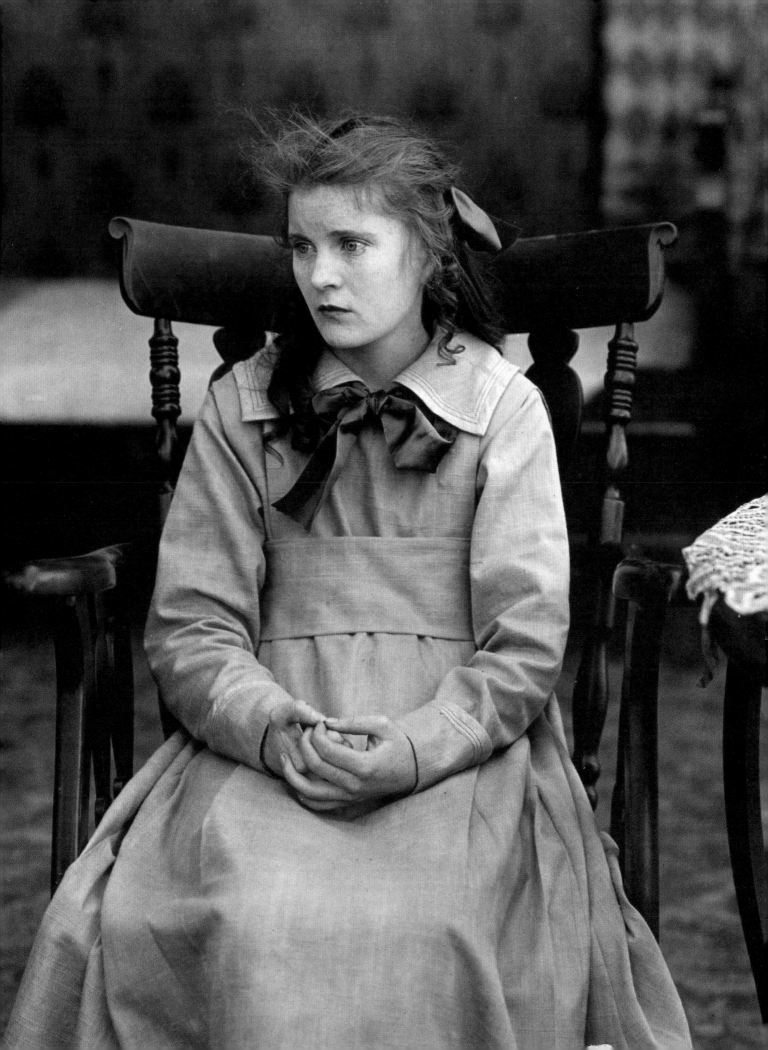

ABOVE Sir Arthur Conan Doyle and family with Mary Pickford, Douglas Fairbanks, Sr., and playwright, Edward Knoblock, 1923

RIGHT Mary Miles Minter in *Moonshine and Honeysuckle*, 1921

OPPOSITE Marion Davies in *Cecilia of the Pink Roses*, 1918

When Sir Arthur Conan Doyle, the creator of Sherlock Holmes, visited Hollywood in 1923, he found a motion picture industry in the first great spurt of financial and myth-making success. Amidst the glamour and illusions (Miss Pickford is seen wearing her costume from her "photoplay" *Rosita*), he must have experienced Hollywood society at its height; the Fairbanks were known as the King and Queen of Hollywood and they ruled from their fabulous mansion, "Pickfair." The society of the talented and rich which gathered around them under the luxurious California sun created a new life style, one which toyed with emblems from the aristocratic traditions of England. "King" Douglas appears dressed for cricket on the playing fields of Eton.

OPPOSITE Corinne Griffith in *Six Days*, 1923

Reginald Denny, 1927

Reginal Denny, born in England, came to Hollywood as a popular leading man with a flair for subtle comedy. *The Leather Pushers* series in which he played a boxer brought him an enthusiastic following which believed itself watching a dashing young American. The advent of sound and the unleashing of Denny's English vowels threw his image off-kilter. While his career never again attained the height of his silent period, he became one of America's favorite Englishmen. Like many early stars, Denny had been well trained in the theatre before beginning a movie career and this enabled him to go on working professionally. Late in his life he played the redoubtable Colonel Pickering in *My Fair Lady* on Broadway; one of his last performances was in *The Country Wife* at the Pasadena Playhouse in 1961-62.

ABOVE Conrad Veidt in *The Cabinet of Dr. Caligari,*
1919

RIGHT Anna Q. Nilsson in *Without Limit,* 1921

OPPOSITE Roscoe "Fatty" Arbuckle and Mabel
Normand in *He Did and He Didn't,* 1916

Fatty Arbuckle worked with Chaplin and made a series of successful slapstick comedies with Mabel Normand. One day, on the set of *Mabel's Strange Predicament,* Chaplin borrowed Arbuckle's oversized pants and shoes for an improvisation, and the little tramp was born. Arbuckle's career was terminated with fearful injustice. Although he was found innocent of a charge of manslaughter, the public would not accept, nor the studios support, his ebullient pranks on screen in the light of what they *felt* about his private life. Arbuckle is but one of many stars who were ruined by fickle moral judgments, a public sentiment which throttles with all the power of the box office.

36

ABOVE Thelma Salter and Laura Sears in *Slumberland*, 1917

LEFT Malcolm McGregor, 1924

OPPOSITE Gladys Brockwell in *Sins of Her Parent*, 1916

Laura Sears! Thelma Salter! Gladys Brockwell! Not quite what we expect for star nomenclature these days. Tony Curtis, Marilyn Monroe, Rip Torn—all as carefully concocted as martinis and publicity releases.

ABOVE Lillian Gish and Mary Alden in *The Lily and the Rose*, 1915

RIGHT Leatrice Joy and Percy Marmont in *The Marriage Cheat*, 1921

OPPOSITE Bessie Love, 1917

This type of mirror shot (Bessie Love) has become somewhat of a cliché through overuse. But it is interesting to note how purely cinematic this shot is, and how stealthily the narrating eye of the camera can approach its subject and capture it, even second hand.

ABOVE Mary Philbin and Lon Chaney in
The Phantom of the Opera, 1925

RIGHT Lars Hanson, 1927

OPPOSITE Dorothy Gish in *Orphans of the Storm,*
1922

rphans of the Storm under the direction
of D.W. Griffith was a fine example of a
good picture being a good commercial product. Griffith rescued a slight and lachrymose
tale by plunging it into the confused strife of
the French Revolution which he depicted with
superb authenticity of detail. Paris was also
the setting for *The Phantom of the Opera,* a
film which had great commercial success.
While it lacked direction on the calibre of
Griffith's, Lon Chaney's brilliant performance,
experimental use of technicolor, and the
gothic atmospherics surrounding the Phantom's mania, make it a remarkable film.

ABOVE Jack Holt and Betty Compson in
Eve's Secret, 1925

LEFT Hope Hampton, 1924

OPPOSITE Joan Crawford and Ramon Novarro in
Across to Singapore, 1928

Joan Crawford was twenty-four when she made this film with a very flirtatious Novarro, the glowing Latin lover of his day. After five relentless decades of unmitigated stardom, Miss Crawford recently had the zest to say, "I love being a celebrity. I never go out on the street unless I expect and anticipate and hope and pray that I'll be recognized... And when somebody says, 'There's Joan Crawford,' I say, 'It sure is!' And I'm very happy about it."

ABOVE AND RIGHT Rudolph Valentino and Vilma Banky in *Son of the Sheik,* 1926

OPPOSITE Rudolph Valentino in *The Four Horsemen of the Apocalypse,* 1921

It is hard to imagine, in these days of Mick Jagger and David Bowie, how this harmless, tasseled horseman could have so outraged and captivated the world of his time. Many regarded him as a degenerating influence on American manhood, while others seemed to find in him an irresistible quality of exotic sensuality; indeed his most famous role made the word "sheik" a synonym for the masterful lover. News of his death was received with such hysteria that several of his fans committed suicide.

OPPOSITE Richard Barthelmess in *The Amateur Gentleman*, 1926

Mary Astor in *Don Juan*, 1926

The use of back lighting, gauzes and soft focus photography created a gentle lumi-nescence to project a highly idealized vision of women. And yet these images from the silent era indicate a more natural sense of feminine beauty than the images from later periods which prided themselves on realism. Here is lovely Mary Astor, her hair unbleached, unsprayed, and uncoiffed for *Don Juan*, the first movie with a fully synchronized musical score.

ABOVE Annette Kellerman in *A Daughter of the Gods*, 1916

RIGHT Gloria Swanson in *Coast of Folly*, 1925

OPPOSITE Buster Keaton in *The Navigator*, 1924

Buster Keaton, stone faced through every improbable acrobatic stunt and situation, was trained in vaudeville, but turned to film in 1917 as a supporting player to Fatty Arbuckle. A series of shorts, written and directed by Keaton, established his reputation as a slapstick comedian.

OPPOSITE Erich Von Stroheim in *The Wedding March*, 1926

Fay Wray in *The Wedding March*, 1926

Von Stroheim gave many notable performances on the screen including the portrayal of a ruthless Prussian Officer, thereby gaining his publicity slogan, ''The Man You Love To Hate.'' But it is his directorial achievements which have become legend. He introduced a hard-nosed realistic vision when dealing with human relationships, and made several films which show the mark of genius even after clumsy studio editing. The recklessness of his spending and his demands on the studios undermined his financial backing, and he had to rely on acting to support himself. His tyrannical profligacies made him the prototype for the clichéd image of a Hollywood director: a maniacal dictator, swanking around the set in riding boots and backing up directives with a swagger stick.

ABOVE Abel Gance in *Napoleon*, 1926

RIGHT Ethel Barrymore and Robert Whittier in
The Call of Her People, 1917

OPPOSITE Evelyn Brent as the Queen of Sheba, 1928

Abel Gance was a French director of such
innovative brilliance that his film *La Roue*
was used by the Moscow Academy to train
their greatest film makers. Jean Cocteau said
of it, "There was cinema before and after *La
Roue* as there is painting before and after
Picasso."

ABOVE Alan Hale and Alla Nazimova in *A Doll's House*, 1922

LEFT Madge Bellamy in *Havoc*, 1925

OPPOSITE Emil Jannings in *The Last Laugh*, 1925

Hollywood has always attracted and courted stars from non-English speaking countries which has brought a refreshing quality of internationalism to the industry. Alla Nazimova, a Russian actress, was one of the first foreigners to become a Hollywood star, and her famous home, The Garden of Allah (she never approved the addition of the "h"), was a meeting place for such international celebrities as Pavlova and Chaliapin, the great Russian bass. Emil Jannings, a German film star who worked in Hollywood during the twenties, is probably best known for his portrayal of the pathetic professor in *The Blue Angel*.

ABOVE *The Battleship Potemkin,* 1925

RIGHT Maria Falconetti in *The Passion of Joan of Arc (La Passion de Jeanne d'Arc),* 1928

OPPOSITE Dolores Del Rio and LeRoy Mason in *Revenge,* 1928

Eisenstein, one of the truly great progenitors of cinema technique, first displayed his mastery in *Battleship Potemkin.* Its most famous sequence, the slaughter of citizens on the Odessa steps by the cossacks, is a terrifying vision of the atrocity. Eisenstein went beyond merely recording events on film; by the use of montage which depended on cutting, juxtaposition of scenes and careful editing, he discovered film as a unique experience in itself.

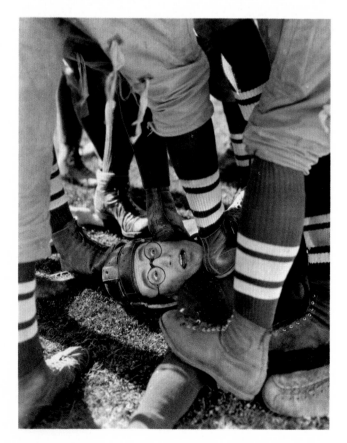

ABOVE Harry Langdon and the inevitable policeman, 1924

LEFT Harold Lloyd in *The Freshman*, 1925

OPPOSITE Jackie Coogan and friend in *The Rag Man*, 1925

Jackie Coogan began wringing tears from stones in *The Kid* which he made at age six with Chaplin. Sceptics were convinced that Coogan's beguiling performance was the result of Chaplin's influence and that genuine talent was lacking. In fact the kid made millions for his studio in film after film.

OPPOSITE Mae Murray in *Circe,* 1924

Pola Negri in *The Cheat,* 1923

As Hollywood became nervous about the growing European film industry, it lured many foreign directors and stars to the United States, among them Pola Negri. Her darkling image, unusual for the time, implied a worldly sophistication which attracted both regular movie goers and intellectuals. Her self-proclaimed love affair with Valentino followed by tumultuous overacting at his funeral dismayed her following and her popularity dwindled.

ABOVE *Ben Hur*, 1926

LEFT Carmel Myers in *Ben Hur*, 1926

OPPOSITE Kathleen Key, Claire McDowell, Francis X. Bushman and Ramon Novarro in *Ben Hur*, 1926

After the carnage when trying to film the famous chariot race in Italy—supposedly more than a hundred horses were killed, not to mention human fatalities—the *Ben Hur* company retreated to Hollywood where a new Circus Maximus was constructed for further filming of the race. Hollywood in all its star-spangled glory turned out to witness the spectacle as part of the crowd. Douglas Fairbanks, Mary Pickford, Lillian Gish, Colleen Moore, Marion Davies and John Gilbert were some of the luminaries who became extras for the fray which was filmed by forty-two cameramen. When finally the film was finished, an M-G-M executive said, "Nothing like it has ever been. Nothing like it will ever be. And nothing like it should have been."

OPPOSITE John Gilbert and Greta Garbo in *Flesh and the Devil*, 1927

John Mack Brown and Greta Garbo in *The Single Standard*, 1929

They speak of the timeless perfection of her face; of her cool silken presence like a flower untouched; and how, when making love, she would cup a man's head in her hands and drink from his lips as though for nourishment.

ABOVE Vilma Banky and Ronald Colman in
The Night of Love, 1927

LEFT Louise Fazenda, 1924

OPPOSITE Myrna Loy, 1927

Here is Myrna Loy looking decollété and
a trifle Victorian seven years before she
became famous as Nora in *The Thin Man.*

ABOVE Bebe Daniels, James Rennie and Ricardo Cortez in *Argentine Love*, 1924

LEFT Neil Hamilton in *The Golden Princess*, 1925

OPPOSITE Clara Bow, 1928

Clara Bow became known as the IT girl after her performance in the movie *It* in 1927. But what was IT? No one seems to quite agree, although it had something to do with restless sensuality tinged, perhaps, with flapper hysteria and a dash of style. Elinor Glyn pronounced that Clara Bow had more IT than anybody else, and besides only three others in Hollywood had IT anyway: Tony Moreno; Rex, the wild stallion; and the doorman at the Ambassador Hotel. Clara loved to ride down Sunset Boulevard in a convertible while surrounded by red chow dogs which matched the color of her hair. Ah, Fitzgerald!

ABOVE Lupe Velez and Douglas Fairbanks, Sr. in
The Gaucho, 1927

RIGHT Douglas Fairbanks, Sr. in *The Black Pirate,*
1926

OPPOSITE Mary Pickford in *The Taming of the Shrew,*
1929

Douglas Fairbanks, the great swashbuckler,
catapulted around his film sets which
reached more and more grandiose proportions until they overwhelmed him. *The Black
Pirate* was a return to the energetic bounce
and more intimate humor of Fairbank's earlier
image. But swashbuckling, alas, takes energy,
and that in turn takes youth. In *The Black Pirate*
Fairbanks used a double for the stunt of sliding
down the sail on a knife, and by the time the
thirties hove in sight—well, swashbuckling
just wasn't what it used to be.

ABOVE AND LEFT John Gilbert and Renee Adoree in *The Big Parade*, 1925

OPPOSITE Alice White, 1928

King Vidor, director of *The Big Parade*, was one of the greatest directors of silent movies. In a business marked by the prodigies and tantrums of his peers, his attitude towards direction was remarkably humble. He felt the director was the medium through which the movie reached the screen, and offered direction in a quiet, undemonstrative fashion. Communication with his actors often involved creation of an atmosphere conducive to the situation. For John Gilbert, he played "Moonlight and Roses" on *The Big Parade* set; for another silent film, Tchaikovsky's Pathétique Symphony provided the emotive theme.

OPPOSITE Mae Busch in *The Unholy Three*, 1925

Alla Nazimova, 1918

ALLA NAZIMOVA

Covers for today's movie magazines typically carry a candid shot of a star under a flurry of hair and dark glasses; perhaps a husband or a lover is drifting in the background—all under a banner headline promising (and not delivering) the inside story of a pending divorce or trumped up scandal.

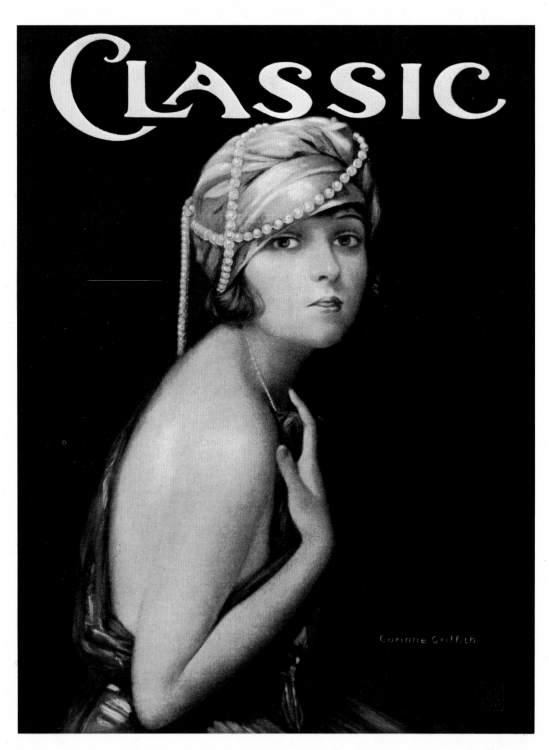

Corinne Griffith, 1921

OPPOSITE Gloria Swanson, 1921

MOTION PICTVRE
CLASSIC

FEBRUARY   25¢

F. Dahl

Barbara La Marr

A BREWSTER PUBLICATION

THE TALKIES

The Thirties and Before

OPPOSITE Barbara La Marr, 1925

OPPOSITE Fanny Brice in *My Man*, 1928

Al Jolson in *The Jazz Singer*, 1927

When Al Jolson got down on his knees to sing "Mammy," sound arrived — and with it a flurry of panic: movies would be ruined, no longer an art form; the new realism of sound would kill off visual imagination. And in truth the camera, now smothered in blimps to silence its clockwork whirrings, was suddenly cumbersome, immobile, devoid of the former grace which Griffith and a host of others had given it. The coming of sound was a revolution (not entirely bloodless) and it took a decade to accommodate its implications. Some silent films continued to be made, but they were no more than outliers. Sound was what people would pay for, and what they would pay for would surely be supplied.

William Bakewell and Helen Twelvetrees in *A Woman of Experience,* 1931

OPPOSITE Phillips Holmes and Nancy Carroll in *Broken Lullaby,* 1932

ABOVE Melvyn Douglas, Herbert Marshall and Marlene Dietrich in *Angel*, 1937

RIGHT Gary Cooper in *Peter Ibbetson*, 1935

OPPOSITE Marlene Dietrich in *Desire*, 1935

The cigarette—ubiquitous in every movie where the very soul of sophistication was sought. Surely future historians will look back on this bizarre habit without comprehension. Only when they see Dietrich on film will their eyes open in wonder, and the delectable pasttime become fashionable once more.

ABOVE Pola Negri with Director, Paul L. Stein, Chief Photographer, Hal Mohr and Assistant Director, E.J. Babille on the set of *A Woman Commands*, 1932

LEFT Jean Parker in *The Ghost Goes West*, 1935

OPPOSITE Anna Sten and Fredric March in *Resurrection*, 1934

The studio blurb printed on the back of this production shot of Pola Negri reads as follows: "When Pola Negri is not working before the camera, she is an interested spectator of scenes in which her fellow players are appearing." Who are they kidding!

ABOVE Johnny Weismuller in *Tarzan Escapes*, 1936

RIGHT Douglas Fairbanks, Sr. in *Mr. Robinson Crusoe*, 1932

OPPOSITE Jon Hall and Dorothy Lamour in *Hurricane*, 1937

Nothing like it had ever been possible in the history of civilization — you could sit in the dreariest small town in the world and make the most exotic, idiotic and compelling fantasies come very nearly true.

ABOVE Bob Kortman, Oliver Hardy, Stan Laurel and Walter Long in *Pardon Us*, 1930

LEFT Wallace Beery and Marie Dressler in
Tugboat Annie, 1933

OPPOSITE Alison Skipworth and W.C. Fields in
If I Had a Million, 1933

The dedicated hater of children and small dogs, the miserable heir to every conceivable distress the flesh can know, venting his tinny spite on whatever cringing aspect of humanity he could momently subvert—no wonder William Claude Fields has become popular again. In our disaster-ridden age, he anticipated nothing else; as we languish before the erroneous computerized bill which like the poor is always with us, and the shriek of the telephone which calls off every act of love, Fields indefatigably puts the record straight. No matter that futility is his inevitable reward.

ABOVE Martha Raye and Andy Devine in *Double or Nothing,* 1938

RIGHT Mary Martin, 1939

OPPOSITE Margo in *Lost Horizon,* 1937

Lost Horizon, based on James Hilton's novel, introduced the term "Shangri La" to describe a Utopian community lost in the Himalayas in Tibet. It was one of many movies based on novels, and it illustrated a trend which increased with the coming of sound wherein movies sought their esthetic form in the art they most closely resembled. Interestingly enough, the trend is now somewhat reversed as many of our best novelists borrow heavily from movie techniques.

Joan Bennett and Francis Lederer in *The Pursuit of Happiness*, 1934

OPPOSITE Helen Twelvetrees, 1929

ABOVE Charlie Chaplin and Bebe Daniels, 1933

RIGHT Olivia De Havilland, 1935

OPPOSITE Ginger Rogers, 1934

Here is Chaplin looking surprisingly dapper and dignified as he always does when not in the character of his tramp or other assorted rogues. The blurbs for these publicity shots, all issued under the guise of giving a glimpse of stars relaxing, point out that Ginger Rogers was "caught in an informal pose" in her living room, while Olivia De Havilland "a-fishing goes" the better to acquire "a sea atmosphere" before shooting her next movie, *Captain Blood*.

Greta Garbo with Cameraman, William Daniels, and Director, Rouben Mamoulian on the set of *Queen Christina*, 1933

Appearance and reality—which is which? This still of Garbo from the final scene of *Queen Christina* is among the most famous in all of film making. What impenetrable secret, what barren waste has her imagination grasped? For this shot, the director asked her to think of *nothing!* Simone de Beauvoir suggests that "Garbo's visage has a kind of emptiness into which anything could be projected."

ABOVE Charlotte Greenwood in *So Long Letty,* 1930

RIGHT Robert Young, 1931

OPPOSITE Laurence Olivier and Merle Oberon in
Wuthering Heights, 1939

Laurence Olivier was first brought to Hollywood in 1933 to play opposite Greta
Garbo in *Queen Christina.* Garbo successfully
opposed his being cast (What an opportunity
lost!) in an attempt to pump some life into the
deflating career of John Gilbert, her usual
leading man, whose voice had recorded with
disastrous results on the crude, sound equipment of the time. It was not until Olivier played
a brilliant Heathcliff in *Wuthering Heights,*
1939, that Hollywood realized what they had
been dicing with.

ABOVE Helen Hayes (left) in *The Sin of Madelon Claudet*, 1931

LEFT Phillips Holmes and Sylvia Sidney in *An American Tragedy*, 1931

OPPOSITE Peter Lorre in *"M"*, 1931

"M" was an intelligent and compassionate attempt to examine the interior workings of a deranged mind. Peter Lorre gave the best performance of his early career as a disturbed child-murderer, finally brought to earth by fellow criminals. He was a hero at once obscenely brutal and capable of drawing sympathy through his suffering.

ABOVE Charles Laughton in *The Private Life of Henry VIII*, 1933

RIGHT Raymond Massey in *The Scarlet Pimpernel*, 1935

OPPOSITE Bette Davis in *Jezebel*, 1938

Charles Laughton's doleful tones and dropsical appearance led to his playing a variety of outcasts, eccentrics and assorted villains. He won an Oscar for his acting in Alexander Korda's *The Private Life of Henry VIII*, and directed the memorable film, *Night of the Hunter* in 1955.

ABOVE Dolores Del Rio and Director, Erle Kenton, on location for *Devil's Playground*, 1937

LEFT Lilli Palmer in *The Great Barrier*, 1937

OPPOSITE Maurice Chevalier, 1932

Almost anyone can look good in a publicity shot. The photographers took exhaustive pains with every aspect of their work, lighting the face for dramatic effects like Rembrandt's, touching-up negatives to conceal blemishes and even changing the contours of the flesh—a little extra weight removed, an ingratiating curve enhanced. The trick, of course, is to look this way at seven in the morning.

ABOVE Bette Davis in *The Private Lives of Elizabeth and Essex,* 1939

RIGHT Vincent Price in *The Private Lives of Elizabeth and Essex,* 1939

OPPOSITE Erroll Flynn in *The Sea Hawk,* 1939

Errol Flynn's real life, complete with youthful wanderings in the South Seas, is even more exotic and bizarre than his life on screen, and much of it he detailed in two autobiographical books, *Beam Ends* and *My Wicked, Wicked Ways.* Mercifully, his indiscretions coincided with his screen image and his reputation was enhanced (an unusual reversal of the public's moral attitude towards stars), although a statutory rape case did cause some alarm. He was cast repeatedly (to his growing and self-destructive disgust) as the contemptuous seducer of women whom he larded with sickening but seemingly irresistible wry charm.

ABOVE John Boles and Gloria Swanson in *Music in the Air,* 1934

LEFT Gary Cooper in *The Adventures of Marco Polo,* 1938

OPPOSITE Claudette Colbert in *The Sign of the Cross,* 1932

Cecil B. DeMille was not a man to miss a story, and when he stumbled on the *Bible* —well, he whacked an entire career out of it, including *The Sign of the Cross.* He made a variety of movies with great success before launching into the spectacular epics with which his name is now synonymous.

Ida Lupino on the set of *The Milky Way*, 1935

OPPOSITE Paul Muni, 1934

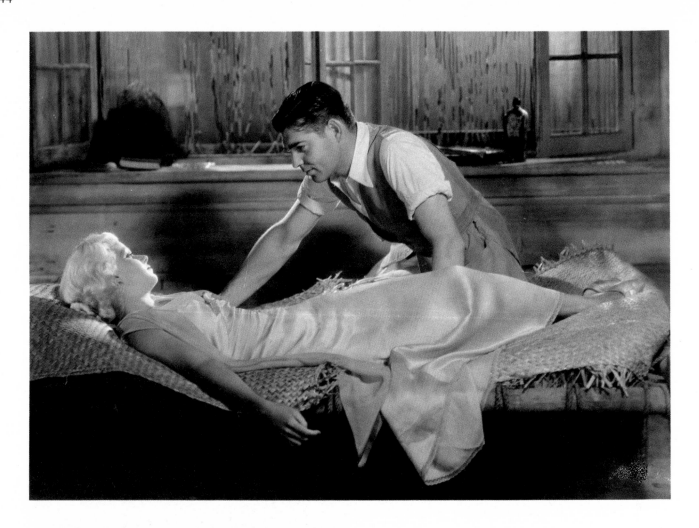

ABOVE AND LEFT Jean Harlow and Clark Gable in *Red Dust*, 1932

OPPOSITE Gary Cooper and Lily Damita in *Fighting Caravans*, 1931

What remarkable men—Cooper and Gable—stars from the beginning to the end of their lengthy careers. Their images were so certain they went untrammeled by their idolatrous public who miraculously never turned against them, neither from boredom nor malice. Of all leading men, these two were the biggest stars with real staying power. Gable was the supreme star of the thirties and forties. Yet he managed to remain a modest, even gracious, man who was insecure enough about his abilities to turn down Rhett Butler in *Gone With The Wind*. Mercifully, he was talked into it.

Ray Milland and Jean Arthur on the set of *Easy Living,* 1937

OPPOSITE Fred MacMurray and Carole Lombard, 1938

ABOVE Florence Eldridge and Miriam Hopkins in *The Story of Temple Drake*, 1932

RIGHT Marjorie Main in *Dead End*, 1937

OPPOSITE Barbara Stanwyck in *Stella Dallas*, 1937

Barbara Stanwyck has become the epitome of the soft-skinned but ruthless American woman. While she does project a certain toughness, she is the victim of an image which has been largely thrust upon her—and, in turn, she has become part of the myth, so staunchly believed in Europe, that American women are harridans who wear the pants. But here she is as Stella Dallas, full of poignant self-sacrifice, in one of the first movies which allowed her to develop a more human character with honest sentiment, someone capable of love as well as sharpshooting.

LEFT Ralph Morgan and Ethel Barrymore in *Rasputin and the Empress*, 1932

BELOW Adolphe Menjou and Virginia Bruce in *The Mighty Barnum*, 1934

OPPOSITE Herman Bing, Alfred Lunt and Lynn Fontanne in *The Guardsman*, 1931

Lunt and Fontanne were at the height of their fame as a theatrical couple during the twenties, and their realistic acting style, considered remarkable for stage work at the time, might well have led them into movie work where a new realism was demanded. In fact they had to be persuaded to film their Broadway hit, *The Guardsman,* their single venture on the screen.

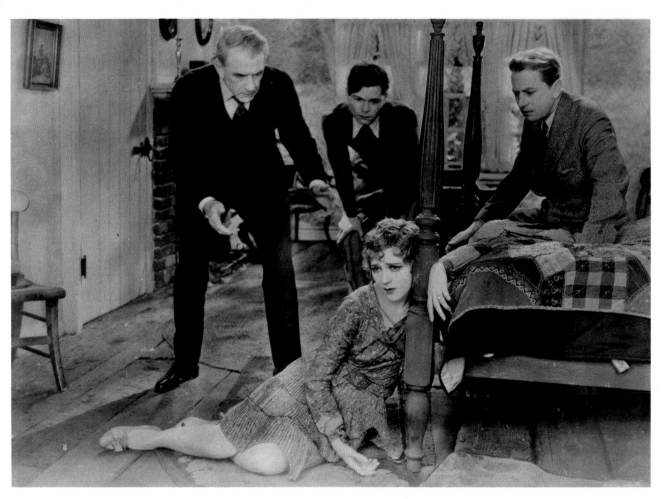

ABOVE George Irving, William Janney, Mary Pickford and Matt Moore in *Coquette*, 1929

RIGHT Gene Raymond, 1933

OPPOSITE Joan Bennett, 1932

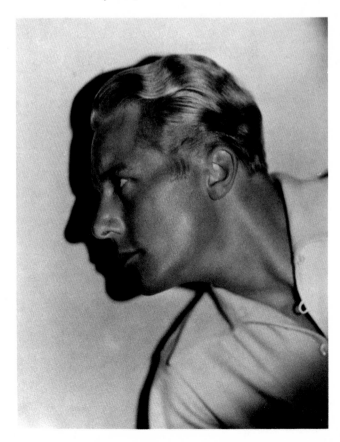

Mary Pickford came out of retirement to make *Coquette* which as a stage play had been a great success for Helen Hayes. While we now tend to think of Mary Pickford as the curly-headed charmer of the silent screen, America's Sweetheart, she was capable of much more than that image suggests. She was a successful producer as well as actress, and along with Fairbanks, Chaplin and Griffith, formed *United Artists*. Her handling of money and shrewd use of her talents made her one of the richest people in the world, while her constant desire for perfection earned her the nickname of "Retake Mary." She received the "Best Actress" Award for *Coquette* in 1928-29, the second year of the Academy Awards.

ABOVE Madeleine Carroll and Henry Fonda in *Blockade*, 1938

LEFT Madeleine Carroll in *Secret Agent*, 1936

OPPOSITE Lew Ayres in *All Quiet on the Western Front*, 1930

All Quiet on the Western Front remains one of the greatest statements on film against war, and helped encourage a new generation of pacifists. The film, based on Erich Maria Remarque's novel and told from the German point of view, is without bombast or heroics. Rather it grapples with the misery and hopelessness of ordinary people enmeshed in the false heroics of the war machine. Its tone and vision approach that of Wilfred Owen's in his great anti-war poem "Strange Meeting:"

I mean the truth untold,
The horror of war, the pity war distilled.

ABOVE Irene Dunne and Charles Boyer in *When Tomorrow Comes*, 1939

LEFT Edward G. Robinson (center) in *Little Caesar*, 1930

OPPOSITE Carole Lombard, 1936

Carole Lombard was first known as Mack Sennett's "Bathing Beauty." She soon became one of the pristine comediennes of the thirties — liberated women who were both glamorous and funny and vastly different to women in pre-depression movies who had played second banana to men or served as mere embellishments. After her marriage to Clark Gable she subordinated her career to his, and was tragically killed in a wartime plane crash.

ABOVE James Cagney and Joan Blondell in
Blonde Crazy, 1931

RIGHT Lupe Velez, 1934

OPPOSITE Eleanor Powell and James Stewart in
Born to Dance, 1936

If these stills don't exactly tumble your eye and send you into hours of dreaming, that's in part because the thirties, and particularly the early thirties, were consumed with churning out sound movies and, of course, musicals. The new medium had to be explored before it could be controlled with the dazzling ease of the Silents. Of course, a film doesn't need too much help from the cameraman when it includes Cole Porter's "I've Got You Under My Skin" and "Easy to Love," two of the hits from *Born to Dance.*

LEFT Dolores Costello and Freddie Bartholomew in *Little Lord Fauntleroy,* 1936

BELOW Claude Rains and Anita Louise in *Anthony Adverse,* 1936

OPPOSITE Norma Shearer in *Smilin' Through,* 1932

Norma Shearer, a bright and hardworking actress, has never been very highly praised by film historians. Nevertheless, she had a significant and somewhat unusual career throughout which she carefully avoided getting typecast. In this she was helped by her husband, Irving Thalberg, one of the great movie moguls, and found herself in the vertiginous position of being able to turn down both *Mrs. Miniver* and *Gone With The Wind* — and given the consequent performances of Greer Garson and Vivien Leigh, she was quite right.

Joel McCrea and Constance Bennett, 1933

OPPOSITE Geraldine Fitzgerald, 1939

ABOVE Nils Asther, Barbara Stanwyck and Walter Connolly in *The Bitter Tea of General Yen*, 1933

LEFT Luise Rainer in *The Good Earth*, 1937

OPPOSITE Anna May Wong in *Limehouse Blues*, 1934

Anna May Wong was one of the most photographed women in Hollywood. Her stunning Oriental beauty led many famous photographers, notably Cecil Beaton and Edward Steichen, to seek her as a model. Unfortunately, she lived at a time when Oriental people were not considered "box office" and as a result her career was limited to supporting roles.

ABOVE Shirley Temple and James Dunn in
Baby Takes a Bow, 1934

RIGHT Jackie Cooper in *Skippy*, 1931

OPPOSITE Dickie Moore and Marlene Dietrich in
Blonde Venus, 1932

Tears, tears, tears! Put a kid on film and there's trauma one way or another. Their consciousness, disarming and seemingly unmasked, shines through with piercing radiance. No wonder the old professional actor let them have it: "Children? They should be painted on the backdrop!"

ABOVE Robert Donat and Elissa Landi in
The Count of Monte Cristo, 1934

LEFT Basil Rathbone in *If I Were King,* 1938

OPPOSITE George Arliss in *Disraeli,* 1930

George Arliss accompanied the famous actress Mrs. Patrick Campbell from England in 1901 and worked with her on the New York stage. Since then his brilliant career as a character actor has linked his name with the many great men he so zestfully portrayed. Here he is as Disraeli, builder of the British Empire, ready to dash onto the greatest stage of all and wrestle with the white man's burden.

ABOVE Leslie Howard in *Romeo and Juliet,* 1936

RIGHT Warner Oland in *The Mysterious Dr. Fu Manchu,* 1929

OPPOSITE Tallulah Bankhead, 1932

Tallulah Bankhead had to make her reputation on the London stage before she could muster her successes in America. She was never well cast by the studios, and her movie career was not spectacular. Her stage career, however, was; as for her life — that's where her greatest talent lay. Her style, her wisecracks, larded with irreligious wit and delivered in her famous husky drawl blew her reputation out of all proportion.

ABOVE Lupino Lane (sitting) and Myrna Loy in *Bride of the Regiment,* 1930

LEFT Anna Neagle in *Victoria the Great,* 1937

OPPOSITE Diana Wynyard and John Barrymore in *Rasputin and the Empress,* 1932

Film is the medium through which our eyes have wandered into the palatial apartments of the truly rich, and drifted through history to linger in the cool presence of royalty. It is a most democratic experience.

It seems unlikely the production of any future movie will provide the great event *Gone With The Wind* did in 1939. The world was a different place, observed through different spectacles. World War II, the Middle East, the paranoid waltz of the superpowers, television—our future distractions were all waiting. By all reports, the production of *Gone With The Wind* caused a frenzy of excitement—and why not? Press leaks alone were sensational: Atlanta burned to the ground before casting was complete; every big star in Hollywood after parts; a fistful of famous directors hired and fired; a two-year search for an unknown Scarlett, and the apparition of the beautiful Vivien Leigh. All this following the outrageous success of Margaret Mitchell's overblown romance which tugged the heart strings and squeezed tears even from stalwart Northerners.

BELOW Thomas Mitchell, Evelyn Keyes, Ann Rutherford, Butterfly McQueen and Hattie McDaniel, 1939

ABOVE Jean Harlow and Robert Taylor in *Personal Property*, 1937

RIGHT Isa Miranda, 1937

OPPOSITE Ginger Rogers and Fred Astaire in *Shall We Dance*, 1937

Fred Astaire and Ginger Rogers—they sparkled with effortless style in the post-depression thirties, dancing on palatial, slick-looking floors untouched by human foot. Astaire's work was a cool perfection—a sublime foil for an age which recognized how hard that was to come by.

ABOVE Elsa Lanchester and Boris Karloff in *Bride of Frankenstein*, 1935

LEFT James Cagney in *A Midsummer Night's Dream*, 1935

OPPOSITE Jack Haley, Judy Garland and Ray Bolger in *The Wizard of Oz*, 1939

Films have perhaps their greatest moments of success when dealing with the fantastic. Extraordinary visions of horror and delight, images of blood-curdling ferocity and winsome loveliness are irresistible, and utterly believable, within the charmed realism of a motion picture.

OPPOSITE Paulette Goddard, 1936

Nancy Carroll, 1931

The term "fan" is derived from the word "fanatic." As an industry developed to pander to this fanaticism, an undertow of cynicism and malicious exposé was inevitable. Notice the spicy headlines promising a frolic around the hero's feet of clay.

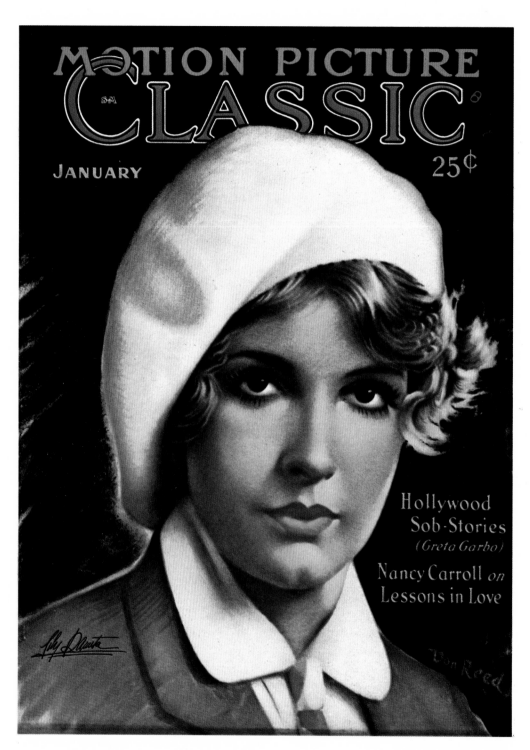

Lily Damita, 1930

OPPOSITE Bette Davis, 1932

MODERN
SCREEN

Bette Davis in *The Bride Came C.O.D.*, 1941

Robert Stack, 1943

Gene Tierney, 1941

Deanna Durbin, 1942

Sterling Hayden, 1941

188

ABOVE Peter Lorre in *Casablanca*, 1942

LEFT Franchot Tone, Thomas Mitchell and Elisha Cook, Jr. in *Dark Waters*, 1944

OPPOSITE Ingrid Bergman and Humphrey Bogart in *Casablanca*, 1942

Casablanca grows more legendary as time passes, and like all legends, it remains inscrutable and certainly inimitable. The extraordinary talent of its international cast, the pity evoked by its Nazi-oppressed setting, the rise of Bogart to super-stardom; none of these elements can quite explain the compelling flavor of *Casablanca*.

ABOVE Jane Darwell and Russell Simpson in
The Grapes of Wrath, 1940

RIGHT Dolores Del Rio in *The Fugitive*, 1947

OPPOSITE Joan Bennett and Gregory Peck in
The Macomber Affair, 1946

The Macomber Affair was based on Ernest
Hemingway's story, ''The Short Happy Life
of Francis Macomber.'' Hollywood is loath to
let a best seller with a name attached drift by,
and Hemingway's was no exception. If only it
had—for the great stylist doesn't film well. He
seems to be a dramatic writer, yet he relies so
heavily on his brand of symbolism that his
lucid descriptions—so often representing a
psychological landscape for his characters—
land up on film as lovely scenery, and the characters, cut suddenly adrift, fall flat. And then
the famous dialogue: it reads like the real
thing; on film it tends to sound like a book.

ABOVE Richard Hart and Lana Turner in *Green Dolphin Street*, 1947

LEFT Rosalind Russell in *Mourning Becomes Electra*, 1947

OPPOSITE Jean Marais and Josette Day in *Beauty and the Beast (La Belle et la Bête)*, 1946

Jean Cocteau, the director of *La Belle et la Bête*, quickly earned himself a reputation as an *enfant terrible* in France. He was strongly anti-establishment, fascinated by the avant garde movements of his time, and bursting with talent which he displayed in several art forms. The young medium of movies was a perfect outlet for his fantasies, and he was intrigued by the magical possibilities within film—a beast could so convincingly turn into a prince, as he aptly demonstrated in this exquisitely visualized film.

Barbara Stanwyck, 1943

OPPOSITE Melvyn Douglas and Greta Garbo in *Two-Faced Woman*, 1941

ABOVE Linda Darnell in *Forever Amber*, 1947

LEFT Agnes Moorehead in *Journey into Fear*, 1942

OPPOSITE Paulette Goddard in *An Ideal Husband*, 1947

Alexander Korda, Hungarian by birth, was the dominant film maker in England during the thirties and forties. He had a dazzling flair for showmanship and netted big names from the worlds of literature and theatre more in the manner of Hollywood than London. The film of Oscar Wilde's *An Ideal Husband* was lavishly costumed with all the turgid detail costumer Cecil Beaton could dream up. And what with a surfeit of extras, exterior shots, and miles of rarefied elegance, poor Wilde's brittle comedy found itself smothered.

ABOVE Gregory Peck and Anne Revere in
Gentleman's Agreement, 1947

RIGHT Helmut Dantine, 1944

OPPOSITE Lucille Ball, 1940

We usually associate Lucille Ball with the raucous folly of her television comedies. But her career began in movies where she was billed as a glamour girl as well as an entertainer—a role she has just returned to in the new film version of *Mame*.

ABOVE Jean Simmons, Martita Hunt and Anthony Wager in *Great Expectations*, 1947

LEFT Margaret Rutherford, Kay Hammond and Rex Harrison in *Blithe Spirit*, 1945

OPPOSITE John Mills in *Great Expectations*, 1947

When Noel Coward wanted the very best editor in England for his films, he simply viewed the current crop of British films and made his choice. It was, of course, David Lean, working his way up through the business, and he went on to direct Coward's *Blithe Spirit* and Dickens' *Great Expectations*. His early directorial choices indicated a literary trend which he has kept in touch with throughout his long career. *Dr. Zhivago* is the most notable example in recent years.

OPPOSITE Danielle Darrieux, 1941

RIGHT Alexis Smith, 1943

BELOW Hedy Lamarr in *White Cargo*, 1942

ABOVE Robert Forsch and Hildegard Knef in *The Murderers are Amongst Us (Die Morder sind Unter Uns.,* 1946

LEFT George Raft in *Christmas Eve,* 1947

OPPOSITE Burt Lancaster in *Brute Force,* 1947

This scene of Burt Lancaster in *Brute Force* calls up an image of his fine performance in *The Birdman of Alcatraz,* 1962. Even though his forte has been in playing uncomplicated characters interpreted with great zest, Lancaster has consistently selected movies with serious themes. He was one of the first actors to set up his own production company.

ABOVE Dorothy Lamour, Bing Crosby and Bob Hope in *Road to Zanzibar,* 1941

RIGHT Patric Knowles and Maureen O'Hara in *A Bill of Divorcement,* 1940

OPPOSITE Jane Russell in *The Outlaw,* 1943

Jane Russell was the choice of billionaire Howard Hughes, a fanciful Pygmalion who hoped to create the most sensational star in the history of movies. Her publicity was so extensive she received 1100 fan letters per week even though her first picture, *The Outlaw,* was not released for three years due to censorship delays. The studio cunningly maintained her popularity with a barrage of 43,000 different photographs.

OPPOSITE Sig Ruman and Harpo Marx in *A Night in Casablanca,* 1946

Groucho Marx and Carmen Miranda in *Copacabana,* 1947

The Marx brothers—there were four of them—started as kids in vaudeville with their mother, Minnie Marx; and they first appeared as a foursome under the winsome title of "The Four Nightingales." Their early films, now preferred by Marx aficionados, did not do particularly well at the box office, and it was Irving Thalberg's interest which carried them to stardom in the late thirties. The irascible Groucho became a well known television personality specializing in the art of insults.

ABOVE Ginette Leclerc in *The Baker's Wife (La Femme du Boulanger)*, 1940

LEFT Anna Neagle, 1940

OPPOSITE Katina Paxinou, Mikhail Rasumny, Gary Cooper and Vladimir Sokoloff in *For Whom the Bell Tolls*, 1943

French Director, Marcel Pagnol's movie, *The Baker's Wife,* has aged but little since it was released in the United States in 1940; indeed this painful and comic story — about a baker's refusal to bake bread for his village until his adulterous wife returns to him — evokes a sense of pity and timelessness which has made it a classic.

234

ABOVE Donald Crisp, Roddy McDowall and Walter Pidgeon in *How Green Was My Valley,* 1941

LEFT Veronica Lake in *Sullivan's Travels,* 1941

OPPOSITE *Mrs. Miniver* with Greer Garson, 1942

Greer Garson received an Academy Award in 1942 for her portrayal of Mrs. Miniver. With all the classic cool those stiff-upper-lipped ladies from Britain are famous for, she adroitly glided from being a society lady twiddling with life to a heroic participant in the Dunkirk rescue during World War II; and for good measure, she pacified the kids with bedtime stories while the blitz raged overhead. Just the ticket for 1942.

ABOVE Herbert Marshall and Bette Davis in *The Little Foxes,* 1941

RIGHT Barbara Stanwyck and Brian Donlevy in *The Great Man's Lady,* 1941

OPPOSITE Vivien Leigh in *That Hamilton Woman,* 1941

The term "Hollywood Star" generally calls up images of blonde hair, dark glasses, poodles and a limousine. In fact, the star system has included actresses as different in type, appeal, and theatrical quality as the three women pictured above. Vivien Leigh was one of the truly great actresses of stage and screen; Bette Davis resisted studio attempts to stereotype her as a glamour puss and developed into an engaging character actress; Barbara Stanwyck found the Western heroine her favorite role. All stars, all successful.

ABOVE *Tulsa* with Susan Hayward and Robert Preston (right), 1949

LEFT Michael Chekhov and Ida Lupino in *In Our Time*, 1944

OPPOSITE On the set of *That Hamilton Woman*, 1941

An unexpected glimpse backstage, a flash of the reality which lurks below, turns out an illusion in itself. But for all the intrigue and glamour of the motion picture industry, a set-up like this takes hours of patient manipulation until, by trial and error, a desired effect is achieved. Actors loll around for hours on end, in make-up and costume, constantly on call while trying not to sweat from heat or drop dead from boredom and fatigue.

243

OPPOSITE Bette Davis and Claude Rains in *Mr. Skeffington*, 1944

Enzo Staiola in *The Bicycle Thief*, 1949

Vittorio De Sica used two non-professional actors to play father and son in *The Bicycle Thief*, a neo-realistic film which was voted among the world's ten best in an international poll conducted in the sixties. The relationship between father and son has a kindly decency which gives the film a universal appeal, while De Sica's restrained direction coupled with the film's poignant ending (which finds the robbed father himself become a thief) achieve a sense of grace.

ABOVE Trevor Howard and Celia Johnson in *Brief Encounter*, 1946

LEFT Charles Boyer and Ingrid Bergman in *Arch of Triumph*, 1948

OPPOSITE Dorothy McGuire in *The Spiral Staircase*, 1946

*T*he *Spiral Staircase* was a Gothic horror story featuring that old stand-by, the homicidal maniac. He was much encouraged by the German director Robert Siodmak and cameraman Nicholas Musuraca whose shadow-ridden stairways and storm-lashed New England scenes were enough to drive anyone potty.

OPPOSITE Marlene Dietrich in *The Flame of New Orleans*, 1941

Gloria Swanson and William Holden in *Sunset Boulevard*, 1949

Her arrogance, her emasculating authority, the insistence of her preening style, make Gloria Swanson the most exaggerated of movie queens. She's kind of fun to think about. Cecil B. DeMille first glimpsed her air of authority when she was an extra on the lot and quickly molded an image for her. Her greatest success was in *Sunset Boulevard* when she played, to perfection, a parody of herself.

Joan Blondell in *Topper Returns*, 1941

OPPOSITE Elizabeth Taylor, 1947

Lauren Bacall, 1945

OPPOSITE Cary Grant, 1943

OPPOSITE Leslie Caron in *Gigi*, 1958

Tyrone Power and Kim Novak in *The Eddy Duchin Story*, 1956

The star-studded, coquettish musical, *Gigi*, reaped nine Academy Awards, plus a special award to co-star Maurice Chevalier for his contribution to the world of entertainment. Leslie Caron created the role of Gigi on the London stage before making the movie in 1958.

ABOVE Paul Newman and Pier Angeli in *Somebody Up There Likes Me*, 1957

LEFT Maria Schell in *The Brothers Karamazov*, 1958

OPPOSITE Marlene Dietrich in *Witness for the Prosecution*, 1957

Marlene Dietrich, the greatest living institution since Queen Victoria. Ever since her fabulous success as naughty Lola in *The Blue Angel*, men have marched to war singing her songs, lusted for her eternal youth, and offered her anything—most of which she has regarded as her just reward. Like all great illusionists, she never gives away her secret. But she constantly reminds you that she has one.

Hardy Kruger in *Bachelor of Hearts*, 1959

OPPOSITE Ava Gardner in *On the Beach*, 1959

OVERLEAF Marilyn Monroe, 1952

ABOVE James Shigeta and Emmanuelle Riva in *Hiroshima, Mon Amour,* 1959

LEFT Richard Basehart in *Moby Dick,* 1956

OPPOSITE Grace Kelly and Clark Gable in *Mogambo,* 1953

Grace Kelly, now Princess Grace of Monaco, proves what you can do in this vale of woe and tears — provided that you are serenely beautiful and have a flair for picking Princes. In *Mogambo,* a remake of the 1932 movie, *Red Dust,* she re-created the role originally played by Mary Astor.

ABOVE Brandon De Wilde, Julie Harris and Ethel Waters in *The Member of the Wedding*, 1953

RIGHT Millie Perkins in *The Diary of Anne Frank*, 1959

OPPOSITE James Dean in *Giant*, 1956

James Dean's sullen sweet looks were backed up by a significant acting talent plus his penchant for getting newspaper coverage as a non-conformist. In the fifties, that was news indeed, and his titillated followers, hooked on the particular combination of perversity and helpless innocence he radiated, idolized him; after his death in a car accident when he was twenty-four, many of his cultists insisted he was still alive and that they had communication with him. In 1957 a short-lived James Dean Memorial Foundation was set up to "translate the force of his legend into constructive channels."

ABOVE Lana Turner and Fernando Lamas in *The Merry Widow*, 1952

LEFT Anne Baxter, 1953

OPPOSITE Ruth Roman, 1951

In the fifties, those *fabulous* fifties, even women coiffed their hair with Brylcreem — or so one might believe. What a greasy decade the Beatles dragged us clear of!

OPPOSITE Spencer Tracy in *The Old Man and the Sea,* 1958

Katharine Hepburn and Humphrey Bogart in *The African Queen,* 1951

Here are three of the great ones, who also happened to be great friends, full of admiration for each other and their work. But it is Tracy who gets the ultimate respect from his colleagues as the greatest natural talent to hit the screen.

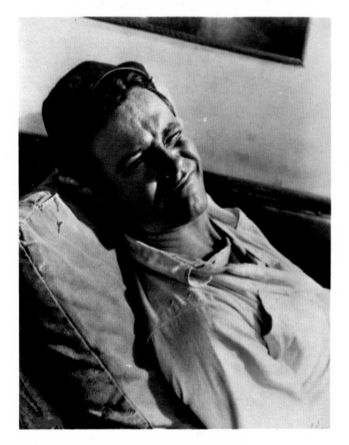

ABOVE Sidney Poitier and Dorothy Dandridge in
Porgy and Bess, 1959

LEFT Jack Lemmon in *Fire Down Below,* 1957

OPPOSITE Rita Hayworth and Aldo Ray (in the
background) in *Miss Sadie Thompson,* 1953

Rita Hayworth is one of the world's most
glamourous and enduring pin-ups. Her
career began in the twenties when she was
aged six, and she remains a presence to be
reckoned with today. Her personal life, which
included marriage to Aly Khan, seems an
embodiment of the romantic image she projected from the screen; a vision of success
which tantalizes the ambitions of generation
after generation.

ABOVE Laurence Harvey and Susan Shentall in
Romeo and Juliet, 1955

RIGHT Mae Marsh and Victor Mature in
The Robe, 1953

OPPOSITE Richard Burton in *The Robe,* 1953

Richard Burton has become something of an enigma, particularly to his fans who early on recognized a great actor in the tradition of Gielgud and Olivier. Then came a slew of dreadful epics which taxed Burton about as heavily as a night of drinking, then marriage to Elizabeth Taylor (always a time-consuming business). The cry of "sold-out to Hollywood" arose. No sooner was the insult offered than Burton turned in a magnificent performance in *Who's Afraid of Virginia Woolf?*, and a Hamlet which many people considered close to definitive. The key perhaps is very simple: Sometimes Mr. Burton is interested, sometimes he is not.

ABOVE Natalie Wood and Tab Hunter in *The Girl He Left Behind*, 1956

RIGHT Lee Remick in *Wild River*, 1959

OPPOSITE Montgomery Clift and Elizabeth Taylor in *A Place in the Sun*, 1951

A glance at these exotically groomed couples immediately calls up comparisons —grade A, grade B. The question always lingers: when will a valid, lively personality shine forth; when will the actor break through the gorgeous facade? Montgomery Clift came to films after a well-established acting career, and he proved to be a star who had a profound influence on his fellow actors. Elizabeth Taylor, the spoiled child of Tinsel Town, might well have disappeared with her aging beauty had not her talents suddenly emerged as an actress in such movies as *Cat on a Hot Tin Roof* and *Who's Afraid of Virginia Woolf?*

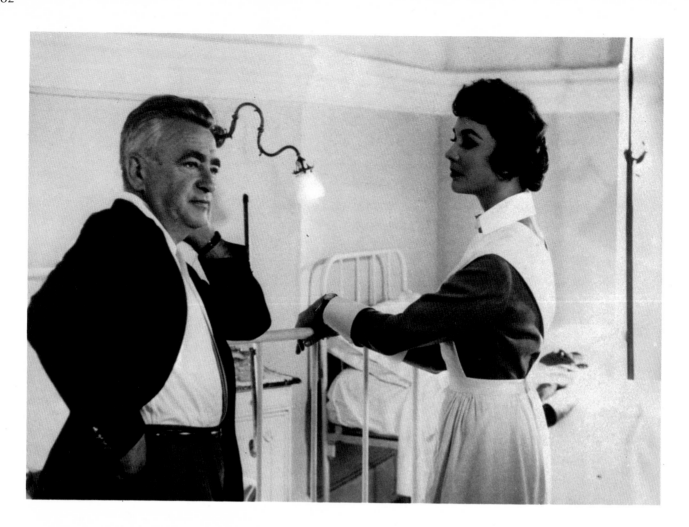

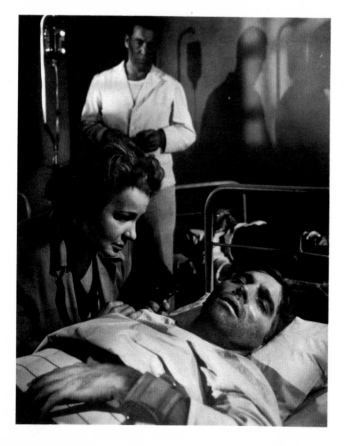

ABOVE Vittorio De Sica and Jennifer Jones in
A Farewell to Arms, 1958

LEFT Shirley Booth and Burt Lancaster in
Come Back Little Sheba, 1953

OPPOSITE Audrey Hepburn in *The Nun's Story*, 1958

Film makers find hospitals irresistible. And why not? They film so very well — each dramatic moment perfectly attended by spellbinding props. Nothing from the bed pan to the scalpel lacks dramatic appeal, while carrying much the same fascination as the artifacts in a medieval torture chamber. And then, there are the nurses. Imagine being swabbed by Audrey Hepburn disguised as a virgin nun!

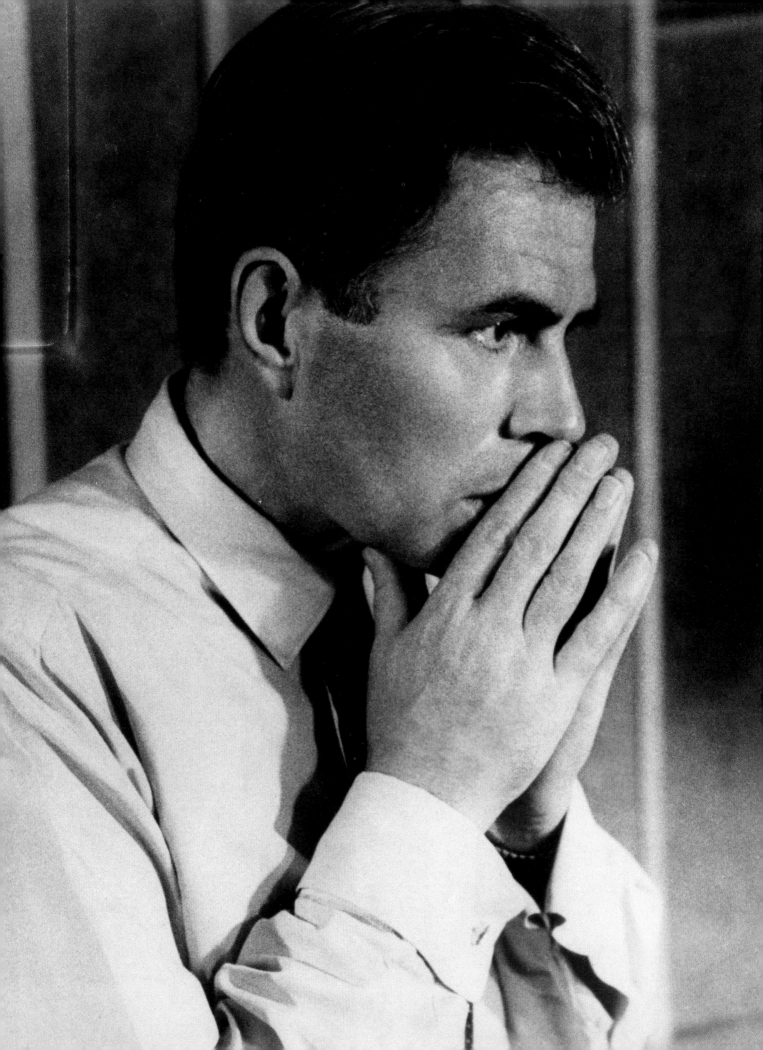

ABOVE Luis Van Rooten, Kirk Douglas and William Bendix in *The Detective Story*, 1951

RIGHT Susan Hayward in *I Want to Live*, 1958

OPPOSITE James Mason in *Cry Terror*, 1958

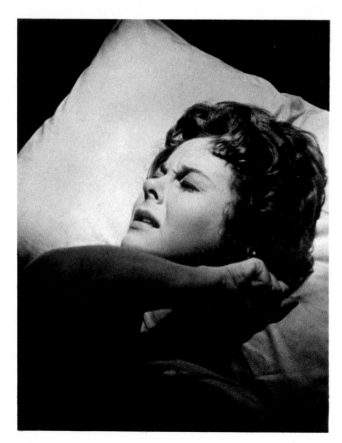

James Mason is another in the line of great English actors, and, like his peers, he received his training on the stage as a character actor before turning his attention to the screen. Perhaps his finest screen performance is as the fastidious and nymphet-loving Humbert Humbert in *Lolita,* 1962.

RIGHT Ingrid Bergman in *Anastasia*, 1956

BELOW Gerard Philipe and Gina Lollobrigida in *Fanfan La Tulipe*, 1951

OPPOSITE Jean Marais in *Orpheus (Orphée)*, 1950

Orphée deals with the moral and social questions besetting a successful artist, interwoven with the lethal strains of the Orpheus legend—here used as a vehicle for Cocteau's private mythology and personal anguish. This still (left) points to Cocteau's unabated intrigue with images of narcissism and appearance versus reality which suffuse this brilliant film.

LEFT Gregory Peck in *The Big Country*, 1958

BELOW Gordon MacRae and Shirley Jones in *Oklahoma*, 1955

OPPOSITE Brigitte Bardot in *The Night Heaven Fell*, 1958

Poor Brigitte, famous for her every aspect except her acting, is one of the most put upon (perhaps willingly) women whose role in life has been to exploit and be exploited by press and public and endless husbands. Truly enough to make the heavens cave in. But at least her resilient image as a free-living and loving person has helped deflect some of the tiresome moral indignation so virulently aimed at sensual enjoyment.

ABOVE Anthony Quinn in *La Strada*, 1954

RIGHT Dirk Bogarde in *Campbell's Kingdom*, 1959

OPPOSITE Giulietta Masina in *La Strada*, 1954

La *Strada*, one of Fellini's most compelling and least decadent fables, assured the director international recognition. The strangely episodic movie, full of tenderness and brutality, is infused with the unearthly innocence of Gelsomina, exquisitely portrayed by Fellini's wife, Giulietta Masina.

ABOVE Harry Belafonte in *The World, Flesh and the Devil,* 1959

LEFT Tom Tryon in *Three Violent People,* 1957

OPPOSITE Joanne Woodward in *The Fugitive Kind,* 1959

Stars like Joanne Woodward and Harry Belafonte were a new breed in the late fifties and early sixties. They were quite prepared to face whatever box office and contractual consequences might follow their well-spoken commitments to political and social change. In addition, Miss Woodward is notable as being a non-star type of the seventies, refusing to invest her personal life with the gold lamé and glitter of the Hollywood myth.

OPPOSITE Marlon Brando and Kim Hunter in *A Streetcar Named Desire*, 1951

Vivien Leigh in *A Streetcar Named Desire*, 1951

Tennessee Williams' plays have not been well transcribed to the screen. Williams has stood by while the woeful states and dire punishments he dishes up for his characters were watered down with happy endings and reprieves to quell the general public. Some bread is better than no bread at all. But his classic *A Streetcar Named Desire*, probably since it deals but little with explicit sex and perversity, escaped unbowdlerized, and remains the most honest and effective film of a Williams play.

OPPOSITE Juliette Greco in *The Sun Also Rises*, 1957

Tab Hunter, 1958

Ava Gardner, 1950

OPPOSITE Suzy Parker, 1959

The Sixties and Seventies

OPPOSITE   Marilyn Monroe on the set of
How to Marry a Millionaire, 1953

ABOVE Richard Harris in *The Bible*, 1966

RIGHT George C. Scott in *The Bible*, 1966

OPPOSITE Raquel Welch in *One Million Years B.C.*, 1966

Some film subjects naturally demand the epithet "pure Hollywood" even before the previews start. Here is Raquel Welch *(One Million Years B.C.)*, a sixties answer to the sinuous Monroe, looking brazenly athletic; sex sneaks in via the talents of her costumer—though who could have imagined *haute couture* rags even one million years ago. And who but Hollywood would dare to offer up *The Bible* in one sitting. Never mind. If you didn't see the movie, surely you can claim to know the book.

ABOVE Rod Steiger in *Doctor Zhivago*, 1965

LEFT Anjanette Comer in *The Appaloosa*, 1966

OPPOSITE *Doctor Zhivago*, 1965

David Lean has directed some of the most romantic films of our time. He seems inspired by overwrought and sympathetic love stories with an adulterous twist. Around such tales, he lavishes mist-soaked mountains, tumultuous storms, perilous seas — every breath-taking vista nature has to give and the camera can take in. Should scenery falter, he turns his camera to the sun and captures lighting effects that painters of the Ascension only dreamed of.

ABOVE Sean Connery and Luciana Paluzzi in *Thunderball*, 1966

LEFT Diana Ross in *Lady Sings the Blues*, 1972

OPPOSITE Robert Redford in *Butch Cassidy and the Sundance Kid*, 1969

Robert Redford belongs to the new breed of handsome, indolent young rebels which includes Peter Fonda and Christopher Jones, and whose progenitor was the much lamented James Dean. *Butch Cassidy and the Sundance Kid* was a highly praised Western with a cleansing seventies' touch — an increasingly law-abiding society forces the heroes into the Bolivian jungles for their violent last acts.

ABOVE Jacques Perrin and Claudia Cardinale in
Girl with a Suitcase, 1961

RIGHT Sophia Loren and Marcello Mastroianni in
Marriage Italian Style, 1964

OPPOSITE Anna Magnani in *The Secret of Santa
Vittoria*, 1969

Italian actresses are admired for a quality of
animal magnetism; their sensuality is that of
the mature woman rather than the sex kitten.
Among them, Anna Magnani was surely the
most compelling. Her acting style was highly
theatrical, but it was backed by an astonishing
vitality which bordered on violence.

318

ABOVE Sarah Miles and Christopher Jones in
Ryan's Daughter, 1970

LEFT Dominique Sanda in *First Love*, 1970

OPPOSITE Paul Newman, 1961

Paul Newman, the husband of actress
Joanne Woodward, is famous in his own
right as a fine actor with a face that sends most
people sprawling. His sorties into the field of
direction have been truly promising, his finest
film to date being *Rachel, Rachel*, which
starred Miss Woodward.

ABOVE Peter O'Toole and Petula Clark in *Goodbye Mr. Chips*, 1969

RIGHT Michael Caine in *The Magus*, 1968

OPPOSITE Julie Christie in *Far from the Madding Crowd*, 1967

Julie Christie, a soft blown English rose, is capable of very fine performances under sensitive direction. Her style shows through particularly well in period costumes; indeed her career is now firmly associated with such movies as *Dr. Zhivago* and *Far from the Madding Crowd*.

ABOVE Melina Mercouri in *Promise at Dawn*, 1969

LEFT Warren Beatty in *McCabe and Mrs. Miller*, 1971

OPPOSITE Mark Lester and Director, Carol Reed, rehearsing for the funeral procession in *Oliver*, 1968

Carol Reed was a leading director during the short, happy life of the British film industry in the forties. Here he is, twiddling tiny Mark Lester in *Oliver*, a musical rehash of Dickens' novel which gave Reed his best box office success.

ABOVE George Chakiris (center) in *West Side Story*, 1961

RIGHT Tom Courtenay in *The Loneliness of the Long Distance Runner*, 1963

OPPOSITE Shirley MacLaine on location for *Sweet Charity*, 1969

Shirley MacLaine, sister of actor Warren Beatty, has a sincere, off-beat quality as a harried working girl, or a cute but unglamorous tomboy. She made a flurry of movies in the late fifties and early sixties, her most distinguished being *The Apartment* which received the Academy Award for Best Picture in 1960.

OPPOSITE Margaret Rutherford in *Murder Most Foul,* 1965

Peter Sellers in *The Pink Panther,* 1963

Mysteries laced with a jigger of crime have proven to be one of England's finer exports — and Margaret Rutherford its most beloved practitioner. She had about her the indomitable qualities of Winston Churchill and the charm of Ariel.

ABOVE Christopher Gable and Twiggy in *The Boy Friend*, 1972

LEFT Martin Potter in *Fellini Satyricon*, 1970

OPPOSITE Vanessa Redgrave in *Isadora*, 1969

Bacchanalian revels are probably more fun —and surely safer—to experience on film than to live through. Still, there is no resisting them; the invitation to the dance is overwhelming.

OPPOSITE Peter O'Toole in *Lawrence of Arabia*, 1962

Claire Bloom in *The Outrage*, 1964

Peter O'Toole is that most roguish of mixtures — the drinking Irishman with a gorgeous set of English vowels. He made a splendid, if overly attractive, Lawrence in *Lawrence of Arabia*, a movie whose 221 minutes of playing time were sauced with David Lean's unfailing vistas and such further delectables as reaped some seven Academy Awards.

Clint Eastwood in *For a Few Dollars More,* 1967

OPPOSITE John Wayne in *True Grit,* 1969

ABOVE Jeanne Moreau and George Hamilton in *Viva Maria*, 1965

RIGHT Bradford Dillman in *Circle of Deception*, 1961

OPPOSITE Laurence Olivier in *Khartoum*, 1966

Laurence Olivier, recently honored in Britain with a life peerage, is presently director of Britain's National Theatre. Of all actors, he is the only one never grudgingly referred to by his peers (if he has any). He is equally adept in film, modern farce, classical tragedy, but it is with the great literary works of the English theatre that his name is forever linked. Of these, he has filmed *Hamlet, Othello, Henry V* and *Richard III* where his villainous but demonically attractive Gloucester is perhaps his greatest characterization on the screen.

OPPOSITE Omar Sharif in *Mayerling,* 1970

Barbra Streisand in *Hello Dolly,* 1968

It is often said that the age of great stars has passed; that actors will not submit to such in-
human exploitation; that the public temperament does not desire them, and above all,
that no star can guarantee a movie's success at the box office the way a Valentino or a Harlow
used to do. Then Barbra Streisand made a smash with *Funny Girl;* movie after movie was
offered to her with the producers' knowledge that she would make it pay.

ABOVE Tatum O'Neal in *Paper Moon*, 1973

LEFT Jack Nicholson in *Five Easy Pieces*, 1970

OPPOSITE Jane Fonda in *They Shoot Horses, Don't They?*, 1969

Director Peter Bogdanovich has a shrewd eye for uniquely American images. He frequently discovers his characters—often a little ragged and run down, in need of a dietary supplement—balanced against an immense skyline, the implacable curve of the New World. A glimpse of this comes across in this still from *Paper Moon,* a sentimental and beguiling movie about the probable relationship between a man and a child, two hucksters in the Mark Twain style, plying gullible widows with a pile of Bibles.

ABOVE Dustin Hoffman, Katharine Ross and
Anne Bancroft in *The Graduate*, 1967

RIGHT Dustin Hoffman in *The Graduate*, 1967

OPPOSITE Mia Farrow in *Rosemary's Baby*, 1968

Just about everyone involved in *The Graduate* achieved heroic status, or at any rate had their reputations well inflated. In industry terms, it was a film to tap the youth market — ages 18-26 — but it captivated a fair handful of thirty-year-olds as well. Just how this movie, so crammed with fashionable attitudes which were being aired in the sixties, will look in ten more years is hard to say; but surely the superb performance of Anne Bancroft is ageless.

342

ABOVE Richard Harris and Rachel Roberts in
This Sporting Life, 1963

LEFT Mary Ure in *Sons and Lovers,* 1960

OPPOSITE Edith Evans in *The Whisperers,* 1966

Edith Evans was made a Dame of the British
Empire in 1949 in recognition of her unfal-
tering and brilliant contributions to theatre.
She has appeared in many movies, and sel-
dom more wonderfully than in *Tom Jones*
when she played the robust and cantanker-
ous termagant, Squire Allworthy's sister.

ABOVE Tippi Hedren in Alfred Hitchcock's
The Birds, 1963

LEFT Keir Dullea in *The Hoodlum Priest,* 1960

OPPOSITE Laurence Harvey and Geraldine Page in
Summer and Smoke, 1961

Alfred Hitchcock, that bizarre and portly Englishman, has sat in Hollywood for at least two generations hatching spine-chilling plots which he then films with the most precise and meticulous working methods imaginable. His taste and flair for the macabre as well as his fascination with crime are particularly English traits which he has never lost track of. The French have been unusually taken with his work, and his influence on a generation of French film makers has been immense.

ABOVE Vivien Leigh in *The Roman Spring of Mrs. Stone,* 1962

RIGHT Jeanne Moreau in *Jovanka and the Others,* 1960

OPPOSITE Marlon Brando in *Last Tango in Paris,* 1973

The greatest stars bring an innate sense of suffering and an extraordinary range of human feeling to the screen — qualities which frequently transcend those of the character portrayed. Even though they are brilliant actors, working within character, their star quality is so unique that we are always happily aware when we are basking in the presence of a Leigh, a Brando, a Moreau.

348

OPPOSITE Charlton Heston in *The Agony and the Ecstasy,* 1965

Marilyn Monroe in *The Misfits,* 1960

In *The Misfits,* a screen play written specifically for Marilyn Monroe by her third husband, Arthur Miller, Monroe gave a performance which introduced dimensions of her personality and acting ability no one had ever seen before, and possibly only Miller and Monroe had truly suspected. She revealed a desperate and overwrought sensitivity which had been carefully concealed in her earlier delicious comedies and sex-ploitation movies.

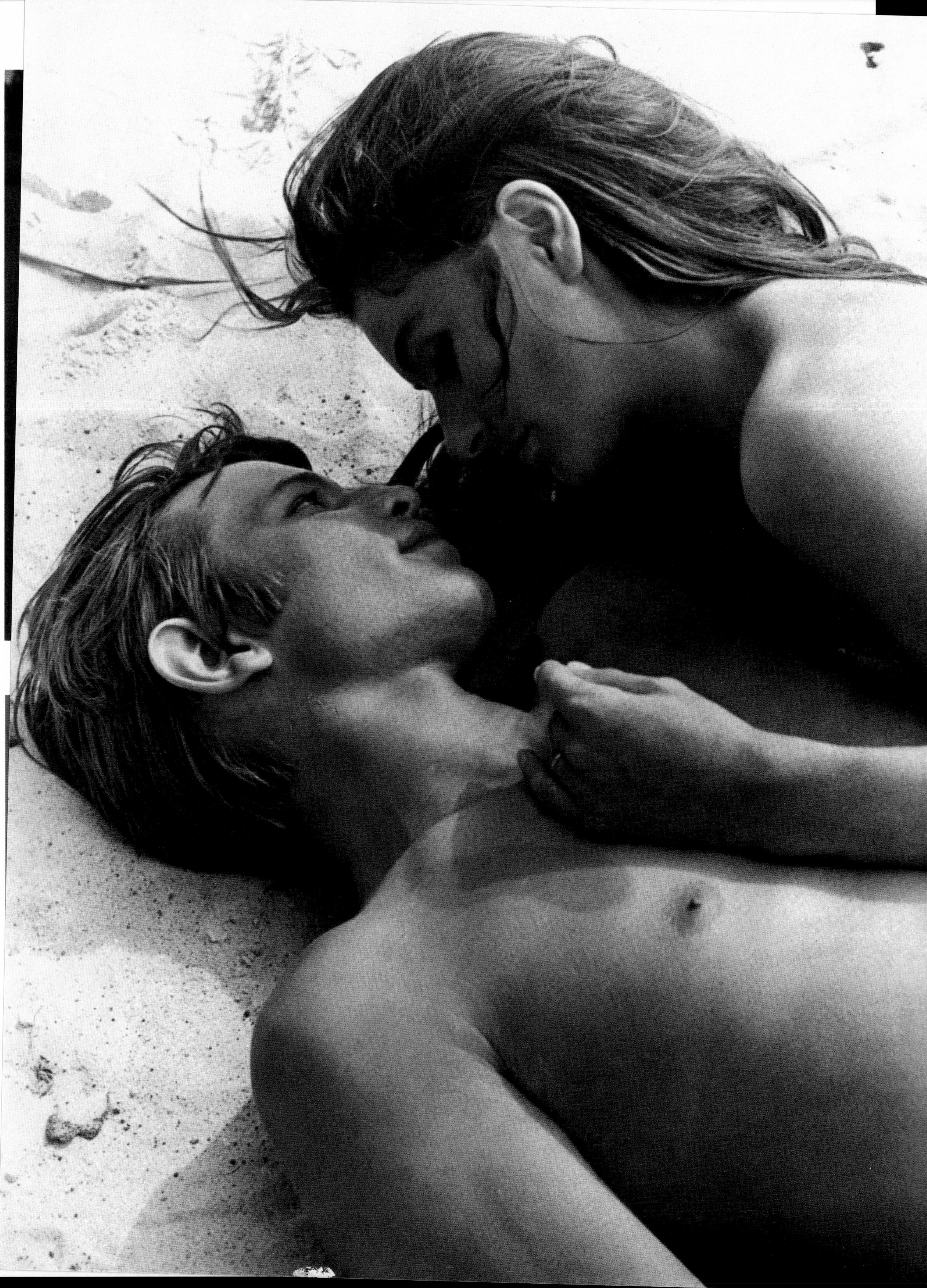

ABOVE Michel Simon and Alain Cohen in
The Two of Us, 1968

RIGHT Jennifer O'Neal in *Summer of '42*, 1970

OPPOSITE Michael York and Anouk Aimee in
Justine, 1969

The complexities of human sexuality have
rarely been directly explored in American
movies, and *Justine* proved no exception
(despite Durrell's best efforts in the novel).
But it remains a subject so tantalizing and dramatic that fortunes have been made by merely
glimpsing it.

354

OPPOSITE Christopher Plummer in *The Royal Hunt of the Sun*, 1969

Katharine Hepburn in *The Trojan Women*, 1971

Katharine Hepburn's continued success has seemingly convinced her of the efficacy of her tough Yankee philosophy, while turning her into something of an American institution—a cliché she would pre-emptorally eschew. And that's the fun of her! She's set for a challenge every day and merrily scales mountain upon mountain. At this point she is so adored by her cohorts—who are legion—any untoward remark might end up in a lynching.

Julie Andrews in *Star*, 1968

OPPOSITE Susannah York in *Tom Jones*, 1963

Catherine Deneuve and Sami Frey in *Manon 70,* 1970

Elizabeth Taylor in *Cleopatra*, 1963

Here are two of perhaps hundreds of publicity pictures taken during the filming of *Cleopatra*. The minute difference between them (if you look closely) is that on this page Miss Taylor is looking vaguely down, and on the page opposite she is looking up.

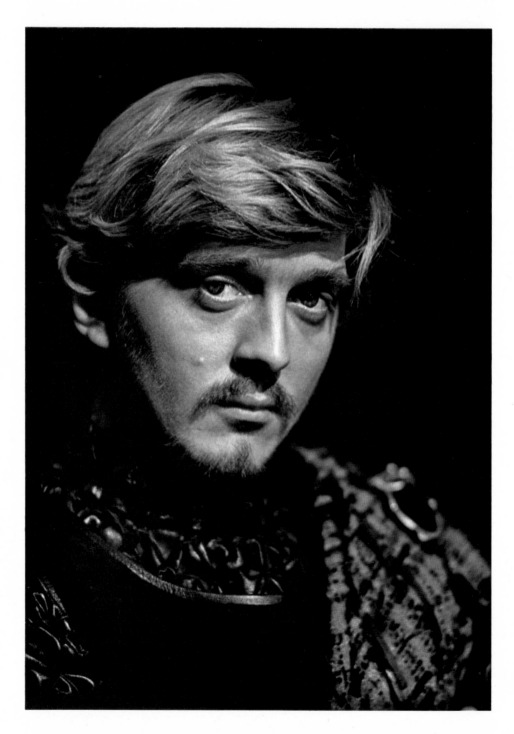

David Hemmings in *Camelot*, 1967

OPPOSITE Sophia Loren in *Lady L*, 1966

OPPOSITE   Anna Magnani in *Secret of Santa Vittoria,* 1969

Yves Montand in *L'aveu,* 1970

Helmut Berger in *The Damned*, 1970

OPPOSITE Audrey Hepburn in *My Fair Lady*, 1964

OPPOSITE Barbara Stanwyck in a recent publicity portrait by John Engstead

Academy Awards

1927-1928

Production: *Wings*
Actor: Emil Jannings in *The Way of All Flesh* and
The Last Command
Actress: Janet Gaynor in *Seventh Heaven, Street Angel*
and *Sunrise*
Direction: Frank Borzage, *Seventh Heaven*
Direction (comedy): Lewis Milestone,
Two Arabian Knights

1928-1929

Production: *Broadway Melody*
Actor: Warner Baxter in *In Old Arizona*
Actress: Mary Pickford in *Coquette*
Direction: Frank Lloyd, *The Divine Lady*

1929-1930

Production: *All Quiet on the Western Front*
Actor: George Arliss in *Disraeli*
Actress: Norma Shearer in *The Divorcée*
Direction: Lewis Milestone, *All Quiet on the Western Front*

1930-1931

Production: *Cimarron*
Actor: Lionel Barrymore in *A Free Soul*
Actress: Marie Dressler in *Min and Bill*
Direction: Norman Taurog, *Skippy*

1931-1932

Production: *Grand Hotel*
Actor: Fredric March in *Dr. Jekyll and Mr. Hyde*
Actress: Helen Hayes in *The Sin of Madelon Claudet*
Direction: Frank Borzage, *Bad Girl*

1932-1933

Production: *Cavalcade*
Actor: Charles Laughton in *The Private Life of Henry VIII*
Actress: Katharine Hepburn in *Morning Glory*
Direction: Frank Lloyd, *Cavalcade*

1934

Production: *It Happened One Night*
Actor: Clark Gable in *It Happened One Night*
Actress: Claudette Colbert in *It Happened One Night*
Direction: Frank Capra, *It Happened One Night*

1935

Production: *Mutiny on the Bounty*
Actor: Victor McLaglen in *The Informer*
Actress: Bette Davis in *Dangerous*
Direction: John Ford, *The Informer*

1936

Production: *The Great Ziegfeld*
Actor: Paul Muni in *The Story of Louis Pasteur*
Actress: Luise Rainer in *The Great Ziegfeld*
Supporting Actor: Walter Brennan in *Come And Get It*
Supporting Actress: Gail Sondergaard in *Anthony Adverse*
Direction: Frank Capra, *Mr. Deeds Goes To Town*

1937

Production: *The Life of Emile Zola*
Actor: Spencer Tracy in *Captains Courageous*
Actress: Luise Rainer in *The Good Earth*
Supporting Actor: Joseph Schildkraut in *The Life of
Emile Zola*
Supporting Actress: Alice Brady in *In Old Chicago*
Direction: Leo McCarey, *The Awful Truth*

1938

Production: *You Can't Take It With You*
Actor: Spencer Tracy in *Boys Town*
Actress: Bette Davis in *Jezebel*
Supporting Actor: Walter Brennan in *Kentucky*
Supporting Actress: Fay Bainter in *Jezebel*
Direction: Frank Capra, *You Can't Take It With You*

1939

Production: *Gone With the Wind*
Actor: Robert Donat in *Goodbye, Mr. Chips*
Actress: Vivien Leigh in *Gone With the Wind*
Supporting Actor: Thomas Mitchell in *Gone With
the Wind*
Supporting Actress: Hattie McDaniel in *Gone With
the Wind*
Direction: Victor Fleming, *Gone With the Wind*

1940

Production: *Rebecca*
Actor: James Stewart in *The Philadelphia Story*
Actress: Ginger Rogers in *Kitty Foyle*
Supporting Actor: Walter Brennan in *The Westerner*
Supporting Actress: Jane Darwell in *The Grapes of Wrath*
Direction: John Ford, *The Grapes of Wrath*

1941

Production: *How Green Was My Valley*
Actor: Gary Cooper in *Sergeant York*
Actress: Joan Fontaine in *Suspicion*
Supporting Actor: Donald Crisp in *How Green Was My Valley*
Supporting Actress: Mary Astor in *The Great Lie*
Direction: John Ford, *How Green Was My Valley*

1942

Production: *Mrs. Miniver*
Actor: James Cagney in *Yankee Doodle Dandy*
Actress: Greer Garson in *Mrs. Miniver*
Supporting Actor: Van Heflin in *Johnny Eager*
Supporting Actress: Teresa Wright in *Mrs. Miniver*
Direction: William Wyler, *Mrs. Miniver*

1943

Production: *Casablanca*
Actor: Paul Lukas in *Watch on the Rhine*
Actress: Jennifer Jones in *The Song of Bernadette*
Supporting Actor: Charles Coburn in *The More the Merrier*
Supporting Actress: Katina Paxinou in *For Whom the Bell Tolls*
Direction: Michael Curtiz, *Casablanca*

1944

Production: *Going My Way*
Actor: Bing Crosby in *Going My Way*
Actress: Ingrid Bergman in *Gaslight*
Supporting Actor: Barry Fitzgerald in *Going My Way*
Supporting Actress: Ethel Barrymore in *None But the Lonely Heart*
Direction: Leo McCarey, *Going My Way*

1945

Production: *The Lost Weekend*
Actor: Ray Milland in *The Lost Weekend*
Actress: Joan Crawford in *Mildred Pierce*
Supporting Actor: James Dunn in *A Tree Grows in Brooklyn*
Supporting Actress: Anne Revere in *National Velvet*
Direction: Billy Wilder, *The Lost Weekend*

1946

Production: *The Best Years of Our Lives*
Actor: Fredric March in *The Best Years of Our Lives*
Actress: Olivia De Havilland in *To Each His Own*
Supporting Actor: Harold Russell in *The Best Years of Our Lives*
Supporting Actress: Anne Baxter in *The Razor's Edge*
Direction: William Wyler, *The Best Years of Our Lives*

1947

Production: *Gentleman's Agreement*
Actor: Ronald Colman in *A Double Life*
Actress: Loretta Young in *The Farmer's Daughter*
Supporting Actor: Edmund Gwenn in *Miracle on 34th Street*
Supporting Actress: Celeste Holm in *Gentleman's Agreement*
Direction: Elia Kazan, *Gentleman's Agreement*

1948

Production: *Hamlet*
Actor: Laurence Olivier in *Hamlet*
Actress: Jane Wyman in *Johnny Belinda*
Supporting Actor: Walter Huston in *The Treasure of Sierra Madre*
Supporting Actress: Claire Trevor in *Key Largo*
Direction: John Huston, *The Treasure of Sierra Madre*
Foreign Language Film: *Monsieur Vincent* (France)

1949

Production: *All the King's Men*
Actor: Broderick Crawford in *All the King's Men*
Actress: Olivia De Havilland in *The Heiress*
Supporting Actor: Dean Jagger in *Twelve O'Clock High*
Supporting Actress: Mercedes McCambridge in *All the King's Men*
Direction: Joseph L. Mankiewicz, *A Letter to Three Wives*
Foreign Language Film: *The Bicycle Thief* (Italy)

1950
Production: *All About Eve*
Actor: Jose Ferrer in *Cyrano de Bergerac*
Actress: Judy Holliday in *Born Yesterday*
Supporting Actor: George Sanders in *All About Eve*
Supporting Actress: Josephine Hull in *Harvey*
Direction: Joseph L. Mankiewicz, *All About Eve*
Foreign Language Film: *The Walls of Malapaga*
  (France-Italy)

1951

Production: *An American in Paris*
Actor: Humphrey Bogart in *The African Queen*
Actress: Vivien Leigh in *A Streetcar Named Desire*
Supporting Actor: Karl Malden in *A Streetcar Named
  Desire*
Supporting Actress: Kim Hunter in *A Streetcar Named
  Desire*
Direction: George Stevens, *A Place in the Sun*
Foreign Language Film: *Rashomon* (Japan)

1952

Production: *The Greatest Show on Earth*
Actor: Gary Cooper in *High Noon*
Actress: Shirley Booth in *Come Back, Little Sheba*
Supporting Actor: Anthony Quinn in *Viva Zapata!*
Supporting Actress: Gloria Grahame in *The Bad and the
  Beautiful*
Direction: John Ford, *The Quiet Man*
Foreign Language Film: *Forbidden Games* (France)

1953

Production: *From Here to Eternity*
Actor: William Holden in *Stalag 17*
Actress: Audrey Hepburn in *Roman Holiday*
Supporting Actor: Frank Sinatra in *From Here to
  Eternity*
Supporting Actress: Donna Reed in *From Here to
  Eternity*
Direction: Fred Zinnemann, *From Here to Eternity*
Foreign Language Film: No Award Presented

1954

Production: *On the Waterfront*
Actor: Marlon Brando in *On the Waterfront*
Actress: Grace Kelly in *The Country Girl*
Supporting Actor: Edmond O'Brien in *The Barefoot
  Contessa*
Supporting Actress: Eva Marie Saint in *On the Waterfront*
Direction: Elia Kazan, *On the Waterfront*
Foreign Language Film: *Gate of Hell* (Japan)

1955

Production: *Marty*
Actor: Ernest Borgnine in *Marty*
Actress: Anna Magnani in *The Rose Tattoo*
Supporting Actor: Jack Lemmon in *Mr. Roberts*
Supporting Actress: Jo Van Fleet in *East of Eden*
Direction: Delbert Mann, *Marty*
Foreign Language Film: *Samurai* (Japan)

1956

Production: *Around the World in 80 Days*
Actor: Yul Brynner in *The King and I*
Actress: Ingrid Bergman in *Anastasia*
Supporting Actor: Anthony Quinn in *Lust for Life*
Supporting Actress: Dorothy Malone in *Written on the
  Wind*
Direction: George Stevens, *Giant*
Foreign Language Film: *La Strada* (Italy)

1957

Production: *The Bridge on the River Kwai*
Actor: Alec Guinness in *The Bridge on the River Kwai*
Actress: Joanne Woodward in *The Three Faces of Eve*
Supporting Actor: Red Buttons in *Sayonara*
Supporting Actress: Miyoshi Umeki in *Sayonara*
Direction: David Lean, *The Bridge on the River Kwai*
Foreign Language Film: *The Nights of Cabiria* (Italy)

1958

Production: *Gigi*
Actor: David Niven in *Separate Tables*
Actress: Susan Hayward in *I Want to Live*
Supporting Actor: Burl Ives in *The Big Country*
Supporting Actress: Wendy Hiller in *Separate Tables*
Direction: Vincente Minnelli, *Gigi*
Foreign Language Film: *My Uncle* (France)

1959

Production: *Ben-Hur*
Actor: Charlton Heston in *Ben-Hur*
Actress: Simone Signoret in *Room at the Top*
Supporting Actor: Hugh Griffith in *Ben-Hur*
Supporting Actress: Shelley Winters in *The Diary of Anne
  Frank*
Direction: William Wyler, *Ben-Hur*
Foreign Language Film: *Black Orpheus* (Brazil-France)

1960

Production: *The Apartment*
Actor: Burt Lancaster in *Elmer Gantry*
Actress: Elizabeth Taylor in *Butterfield 8*
Supporting Actor: Peter Ustinov in *Spartacus*
Supporting Actress: Shirley Jones in *Elmer Gantry*
Direction: Billy Wilder, *The Apartment*
Foreign Language Film: *The Virgin Spring* (Sweden)

1961

Production: *West Side Story*
Actor: Maximilian Schell in *Judgment at Nuremberg*
Actress: Sophia Loren in *Two Women*
Supporting Actor: George Chakiris in *West Side Story*
Supporting Actress: Rita Moreno in *West Side Story*
Direction: Robert Wise and Jerome Robbins, *West Side Story*
Foreign Language Film: *Through A Glass Darkly* (Sweden)

1962

Production: *Lawrence of Arabia*
Actor: Gregory Peck in *To Kill a Mockingbird*
Actress: Anne Bancroft in *The Miracle Worker*
Supporting Actor: Ed Begley in *Sweet Bird of Youth*
Supporting Actress: Patty Duke in *The Miracle Worker*
Direction: David Lean, *Lawrence of Arabia*
Foreign Language Film: *Sundays and Cybele* (France)

1963

Production: *Tom Jones*
Actor: Sidney Poitier in *Lilies of the Field*
Actress: Patricia Neal in *Hud*
Supporting Actor: Melvyn Douglas in *Hud*
Supporting Actress: Margaret Rutherford in *The V.I.P.s*
Direction: Tony Richardson, *Tom Jones*
Foreign Language Film: *8½* (Italy)

1964

Production: *My Fair Lady*
Actor: Rex Harrison in *My Fair Lady*
Actress: Julie Andrews in *Mary Poppins*
Supporting Actor: Peter Ustinov in *Topkapi*
Supporting Actress: Lila Kedrova in *Zorba the Greek*
Direction: George Cukor, *My Fair Lady*
Foreign Language Film: *Yesterday, Today and Tomorrow* (Italy)

1965

Production: *The Sound of Music*
Actor: Lee Marvin in *Cat Ballou*
Actress: Julie Christie in *Darling*
Supporting Actor: Martin Balsam in *A Thousand Clowns*
Supporting Actress: Shelley Winters in *A Patch of Blue*
Direction: Robert Wise, *The Sound of Music*
Foreign Language Film: *The Shop on Main Street* (Czechoslovakia)

1966

Production: *A Man for All Seasons*
Actor: Paul Scofield in *A Man for All Seasons*
Actress: Elizabeth Taylor in *Who's Afraid of Virginia Woolf?*
Supporting Actor: Walter Matthau in *The Fortune Cookie*
Supporting Actress: Sandy Dennis in *Who's Afraid of Virginia Woolf?*
Direction: Fred Zinnemann, *A Man for All Seasons*
Foreign Language Film: *A Man and a Woman* (France)

1967

Production: *In the Heat of the Night*
Actor: Rod Steiger in *In the Heat of the Night*
Actress: Katharine Hepburn in *Guess Who's Coming to Dinner?*
Supporting Actor: George Kennedy in *Cool Hand Luke*
Supporting Actress: Estelle Parsons in *Bonnie and Clyde*
Direction: Mike Nichols, *The Graduate*
Foreign Language Film: *Closely Watched Trains* (Czechoslovakia)

1968

Production: *Oliver*
Actor: Cliff Robertson in *Charly*
Actress: Katharine Hepburn in *The Lion in Winter* and Barbra Streisand in *Funny Girl*
Supporting Actor: Jack Albertson in *The Subject Was Roses*
Supporting Actress: Ruth Gordon in *Rosemary's Baby*
Direction: Carol Reed, *Oliver*
Foreign Language Film: *War and Peace* (Russia)

1969

Production: *Midnight Cowboy*
Actor: John Wayne in *True Grit*
Actress: Maggie Smith in *The Prime of Miss Jean Brodie*
Supporting Actor: Gig Young in *They Shoot Horses, Don't They?*
Supporting Actress: Goldie Hawn in *Cactus Flower*
Direction: John Schlesinger, *Midnight Cowboy*
Foreign Language Film: *"Z"* (Costa-Gavras)

1970

Production: *Patton*
Actor: George C. Scott in *Patton*
Actress: Glenda Jackson in *Women in Love*
Supporting Actor: John Mills in *Ryan's Daughter*
Supporting Actress: Helen Hayes in *Airport*
Direction: Franklin J. Schaffner, *Patton*
Foreign Language Film: *Investigation of a Citizen Above Suspicion* (Italy)

1971

Production: *The French Connection*
Actor: Gene Hackman in *The French Connection*
Actress: Jane Fonda in *Klute*
Supporting Actor: Ben Johnson in *The Last Picture Show*
Supporting Actress: Cloris Leachman in *The Last Picture Show*
Direction: William Friedkin, *The French Connection*
Foreign Language Film: *The Garden of the Finzi Contini* (Italy)

1972

Production: *The Godfather*
Actor: Marlan Brando in *The Godfather*
Actress: Liza Minnelli in *Cabaret*
Supporting Actor: Joel Grey in *Cabaret*
Supporting Actress: Eileen Heckart in *Butterflies Are Free*
Direction: Bob Fosse, *Cabaret*
Foreign Language Film: *The Discreet Charm of the Bourgeoisie* (France)

1973

Production: *The Sting*
Actor: Jack Lemmon in *Save the Tiger*
Actress: Glenda Jackson in *A Touch of Class*
Supporting Actor: John Houseman in *Paper Chase*
Supporting Actress: Tatum O'Neal in *Paper Moon*
Direction: George Roy Hill, *The Sting*
Foreign Language Film: *Day for Night* (France)

Index

Across to Singapore, 43
Adams, Kathryn, 24
Adoration, 92
Adventures of Marco Polo, The, 132
African Queen, The, 269
Aimee, Anouk, 352
Agony and the Ecstasy, The, 349
Alden, Mary, 39
Alibi Ike, 143
All Quiet on the Western Front, 155
Amateur Gentleman, 47
American Tragedy, An, 124
Anastasia, 287
Andrews, Julie, 357
Angel, 107
Angeli, Pier, 256
An Ideal Husband, 201
Anthony Adverse, 160
Appaloosa, The, 312
Arbuckle, Roscoe "Fatty", 34
Arch of Triumph, 244
Argentine Love, 74
Arlen, Richard, 69
Arliss, George, 169
Armetta, Henry, 84
Arthur, Jean, 147
Astaire, Fred, 176
Asther, Nils, 164
Astor, Mary, 46, 89
Ayres, Lew, 155
Babille, E.J., 108
Baby Takes A Bow, 167
Bacall, Lauren, 250
Bachelor of Hearts, 259
Baker's Wife, The, 232
Bakewell, William, 104
Ball, Lucille, 202
Bancroft, Anne, 341, 351
Bankhead, Tallulah, 170
Banky, Vilma, 45, 66
Bara, Theda, 21
Bardot, Brigitte, 289
Barrault, Jean-Louis, 222
Barrier, Edgar, 223
Barriscale, Bessie, 27
Barrymore, Ethel, 53, 150
Barrymore, John, 24, 87, 173
Barthelmess, Richard, 47
Bartholomew, Freddie, 160
Basehart, Richard, 262
Battleship Potemkin, The, 57
Baxter, Anne, 266
Baxter, Warner, 73
Beatty, Warren, 322
Beauty and the Beast (La Belle et la Bête), 193

Beery, Wallace, 112
Belafonte, Harry, 292
Bellamy, Madge, 54
Belmondo, Jean-Paul, 298
Beloved Rogue, The, 87
Bendix, William, 228, 285
Ben Hur, 62, 63
Bennett, Constance, 163
Bennett, Enid, 27
Bennett, Joan, 116, 152, 190
Berger, Helmut, 366
Bergman, Ingrid, 189, 226, 244, 287, 350
Bernhardt, Sarah, 17
Bible, The, 311
Bicycle Thief, The, 243
Big Country, The, 288
Big Parade, The, 80
Bill of Divorcement, A, 217
Bing, Herman, 151
Binney, Constance, 24
Birds, The, 344
Birth of a Nation, 18
Bitter Tea of General Yen, The, 164
Black Pirate, The, 79
Blithe Spirit, 204
Blockade, 154
Blonde Crazy, 159
Blonde Venus, 166
Blondell, Joan, 159, 248
Bloom, Claire, 331
Bogarde, Dirk, 291
Bogart, Humphrey, 189, 229, 231, 269
Boles, John, 132, 138
Bolger, Ray, 179
Booth, Shirley, 282
Borden, Olive, 93
Born to Dance, 158
Bow, Clara, 69, 75
Boyer, Charles, 156, 244
Boy Friend, The, 328
Brando, Marlon, 275, 294, 346
Breathless (A Bout de Souffle), 298, 299
Brent, Evelyn, 52
Brice, Fanny, 102
Bride Came C.O.D., The, 186
Bride of Frankenstein, 178
Bride of the Regiment, 172
Brief Encounter, 244
Briggs, Jack, 227
Brockwell, Gladys, 37
Broken Lullaby, 105
Bronson, Betty, 71
Brook, Clive, 72, 139
Brothers Karamazov, The, 256
Brown, Joe E., 143
Brown, John Mack, 65

Bruce, Virginia, 150
Brute Force, 209
Burton, Richard, 272
Busch, Mae, 96
Bushman, Francis X., 63
Butch Cassidy and the Sundance Kid, 315
Cabinet of Dr. Caligari, The, 35
Cagney, James, 159, 178
Caine, Michael, 321
Call of Her People, The, 53
Camelot, 362
Camille, 73
Campbell's Kingdom, 291
Cardinale, Claudia, 317
Caron, Leslie, 254
Carroll, Madeleine, 154
Carroll, Nancy, 105, 181
Casablanca, 188, 189
Casares, Maria, 222
Cecilia of the Pink Roses, 30
Chakiris, George, 325
Chaney, Lon, 41, 85
Chaplin, Charles, 94, 95, 119
Cheat, The, 61
Chekhov, Michael, 240
Cherkassov, Nikolai, 196
Chevalier, Maurice, 129
Children of Paradise (Les Enfants du Paradis), 222
Christie, Julie, 320
Christmas Eve, 208
Circe, 60
Circle of Deception, 335
Citizen Kane, 214
Clark, Petula, 321
Cleopatra, 360, 361
Clift, Montgomery, 224, 280
Coast of Folly, 49
Coburn, Robert, 300
Cohen, Alain, 353
Colbert, Claudette, 133
Colman, Ronald, 66
Collyer, June, 82
Colorado Territory, 230
Come Back Little Sheba, 282
Comer, Anjanette, 312
Comingore, Dorothy, 214
Compson, Betty, 42
Connery, Sean, 314
Connolly, Walter, 164
Constant Nymph, The, 212
Coogan, Jackie, 59
Cook, Jr., Elisha, 188
Cooper, Gary, 107, 132, 145, 233
Cooper, Gladys, 296
Cooper, Jackie, 167
Copacabana, 218
Coquette, 153

Corn is Green, The, 210
Cortez, Ricardo, 74
Costello, Dolores, 160
Count of Monte Cristo, The, 168
Courtenay, Tom, 325
Crawford, Joan, 43, 140, 184, 238, 239
Crisp, Donald, 234
Crosby, Bing, 217
Cry Terror, 284
Dall, John, 210
Damita, Lily, 145, 182
Damned, The, 366
Dandridge, Dorothy, 270
Daniels, Bebe, 74, 119
Daniels, William, 120
Dantine, Helmut, 203
Dark Waters, 188
Darrieux, Danielle, 206
Darwell, Jane, 191
Darnell, Linda, 200
Daughter of the Gods, A, 49
Davies, Marion, 30
Davis, Bette, 126, 131, 141, 183, 186, 237, 242
Day, Josette, 193
Day, Laraine, 220
Dead End, 149
Dean, James, 264
De Carlo, Yvonne, 195
De Havilland, Olivia, 119, 224
Del Rio, Dolores, 56, 128, 191
Deneuve, Catherine, 358, 359
Denny, Reginald, 32
De Sica, Vittorio, 282
Desire, 106
Detective Story, 285
Devil's Playground, 128
Devine, Andy, 115
De Wilde, Brandon, 265
Diary of Anne Frank, The, 265
Dietrich, Marlene, 106, 107, 166, 247, 257, 296
Dillman, Bradford, 335
Disraeli, 169
Divine Lady, The, 89
Doctor Zhivago, 312, 313
Doll's House, A, 54
Donat, Robert, 168
Don Juan, 46
Donlevy, Brian, 237
Doro, Marie, 25
Double or Nothing, 115
Douglas, Kirk, 285
Douglas, Melvyn, 107, 198
Dove, Billie, 92
Down to the Sea in Ships, 213
Doyle, Sir Arthur Conan, 31
Dressler, Marie, 89, 112

Dullea, Keir, 344
Dunn, James, 167
Dunne, Irene, 156
Durante, Jimmy, 195
Durbin, Deanna, 187
Eastwood, Clint, 332
Easy Living, 147
Eddy Duchin Story, The, 255
Ekerot, Bengt, 277
Eldridge, Florence, 149
Eternal Love, 87
Evans, Edith, 343
Eve's Secret, 42
Experiment Perilous, 211
Face at the Window, The, 93
Fairbanks, Sr., Douglas, 31, 79, 111
Falconetti, Maria, 57
Fanfan La Tulipe, 287
Farewell to Arms, A, 282
Far from the Madding Crowd, 320
Farrell, Charles, 86
Farrow, Mia, 340
Fazenda, Louise, 66
Fellini Satyricon, 328
Field, Betty, 223
Fields, W.C., 113
Fighting Caravans, 145
Fig Leaves, 93
Fire Down Below, 270
First Love, 318
Fitzgerald, Geraldine, 162
Five Easy Pieces, 338
Flame of New Orleans, 247
Flesh and Fantasy, 223
Flesh and the Devil, 64
Flynn, Errol, 130, 228
Fonda, Henry, 154, 274
Fonda, Jane, 339
Fontaine, Joan, 212, 215
Fontanne, Lynn, 151
Footsteps in the Fog, 279
For a Few Dollars More, 332
Forever Amber, 200
For Whom the Bell Tolls, 226, 233
Forsch, Robert, 208
Four Horsemen of the Apocalypse,
Foxes of Harrow, The, 224
Francis, Kay, 137
Frazer, Richard, 227
Frederick, Pauline, 93
Freshman, The, 58
Fresnay, Pierre, 210
Frey, Sami, 359
Fugitive Kind, The, 293
Fugitive, The, 191
Gabin, Jean, 140
Gable, Christopher, 328
Gable, Clark, 144, 175, 263
Gabor, Zsa Zsa, 278

Gance, Abel, 53
Garbo, Greta, 64, 65, 120, 121, 198
Gardner, Ava, 258, 306
Garfield, John, 238
Garland, Judy, 179
Garson, Greer, 235
Gaucho, The, 79
Gaynor, Janet, 77, 84
Genevieve, 297
Gentleman's Agreement, 203
Ghost Goes West, The, 108
Giant, 264
Gigi, 254
Gilbert, John, 64, 80, 88
Girl He Left Behind, The, 281
Girl With a Suitcase, 317
Gish, Dorothy, 40
Gish, Lillian, 39, 88
Goddard, Paulette, 95, 180, 201
Golden Bed, The, 73
Golden Princess, The, 74
Gold Rush, The, 94, 95
Gone With the Wind, 174, 175
Goodbye Again, 350
Goodbye Mr. Chips, 321
Good Earth, The, 164
Graduate, The, 341
Grant, Cary, 215, 251
Grapes of Wrath, The, 191
Great Barrier, The, 128
Great Expectations, 204, 205
Great Man's Lady, The, 237
Great Train Robbery, The, 12
Greco, Juliette, 303
Green Dolphin Street, 192
Greenwood, Charlotte, 123
Griffith, Corinne, 33, 89, 98
Guardsman, The, 151
Hale, Alan, 54
Haley, Jack, 179
Hall, Jon, 110
Halliday, John, 139
Hamilton, George, 335
Hamlet, 197
Hammond, Kay, 204
Hampton, Hope, 42
Hanson, Lars, 41
Harding, Ann, 138
Hardy, Oliver, 112
Harlow, Jean, 144, 177
Harris, Julie, 265
Harris, Richard, 192
Harrison, Rex, 204
Hart, Richard, 192
Hart, William S., 26
Harvey, Laurence, 273, 345
Hater of Men, 27
Havoc, 54
Hayden, Sterling, 187

Hayes, Helen, 124
Hayward, Susan, 240, 285
Hayworth, Rita, 271
He Did and He Didn't, 34
Hedren, Tippi, 344
Heflin, Van, 225
Heiress, The, 224
Hello Dolly, 336
Hemmings, David, 362
Henreid, Paul, 227
Hepburn, Audrey, 283, 367
Hepburn, Katharine, 269, 354
Heston, Charlton, 349
Hiroshima, Mon Amour, 262
Hoffman, Dustin, 341
Holden, William, 246
Holmes, Phillips, 105, 124
Holt, Jack, 42
Holt, Tim, 231
Hoodlum Priest, The, 344
Hope, Bob, 217
Hopkins, Miriam, 149
Hostages, 228
Howard, Leslie, 141, 171
Howard, Trevor, 227, 244
How to Marry a Millionaire, 308
How Green Was My Valley, 234
Hudson, Rock, 305
Hull, Henry, 228
Humoresque, 238, 239
Hunt, Martita, 204
Hunter, Kim, 294
Hunter, Tab, 281, 302
Hurricane, 110
Huston, Walter, 231
I Died A Thousand Times, 274
If I Had A Million, 113
If I Were King, 168
I'm No Angel, 142
In Our Time, 240
Irving, George, 153
Irwin, May, 8
Isadora, 329
Ivan the Terrible, 196
I Want to Live, 285
Janney, William, 153
Jannings, Emil, 55
Jazz Singer, The, 103
Jezebel, 126
Joan of Paris, 227
Johnson, Celia, 244
Jolson, Al, 103
Jones, Christopher, 318
Jones, Jennifer, 225, 282
Jones, Shirley, 288
Journey into Fear, 200
Jovanka and the Others, 347
Joy, Leatrice, 39
Justine, 352

Karloff, Boris, 178
Keaton, Buster, 48
Kellerman, Annette, 49
Kelly, Grace, 263
Kendall, Kay, 297
Kenton, Erle, 128
Kerr, Deborah, 296, 304
Key, Kathleen, 63
Keyes, Evelyn, 174
Khartoum, 334
King and I, The, 304
Kiss, The, 8
Knef, Hildegard, 208
Knoblock, Edward, 31
Knowles, Patric, 217
Kortman, Bob, 112
Kruger, Hardy, 259
La Boheme, 88
Ladd, Alan, 227
Lady L, 363
Lady Sings the Blues, 314
Lake, Veronica, 234
LaMarr, Barbara, 100
Lamarr, Hedy, 207, 211
Lamas, Fernando, 266
Lamour, Dorothy, 110, 217
Landi, Elissa, 168
Lane, Lupino, 172
Lancaster, Burt, 209, 282
Lanchester, Elsa, 178
Langdon, Harry, 58
La Rocque, Rod, 90
Last Laugh, The, 55
La Strada, 290, 291
Last Tango in Paris, 346
Laugh Clown Laugh, 85
Laughton, Charles, 127
Laurel, Stan, 112
L'aveu, 365
Law of Men, The, 27
Lawrence, Florence, 14
Lawrence of Arabia, 330
Leclerc, Ginette, 232
Lederer, Francis, 116
Lee, Lila, 84
Leigh, Vivien, 174, 175, 236, 295, 347
Lemmon, Jack, 270
Lester, Mark, 323
Life of Vergie Winters, The, 138
Lilac Time, 68
Lily and the Rose, The, 39
Limehouse Blues, 165
Little Caesar, 156
Little Foxes, The, 237
Little Lord Fauntleroy, 160
Lloyd, Harold, 58
Locket, The, 220
Lollobrigida, Gina, 287

Lombard, Carole, 146, 157
Loneliness of the Long Distance Runner, 325
Long, Walter, 112
Loren, Sophia, 317, 363
Lorre, Peter, 125, 188
Lost Horizon, 114
Louise, Anita, 160
Love, Bessie, 38
Loy, Myrna, 67, 136, 172
Lunt, Alfred, 151
Lupino, Ida, 135, 240
Lydia, 213
"M", 125
Mackaill, Dorothy, 93
MacLaine, Shirley, 324
MacMurray, Fred, 146
Macomber Affair, The, 190
MacRae, Gordon, 288
Madame Bovary, 225
Magnani, Anna, 316, 364
Magus, The, 321
Main, Marjorie, 149
Mamoulian, Rouben, 120
Mandalay, 137
Manon, 70, 358, 359
Marais, Jean, 193, 286
March, Fredric, 109
Margo, 114
Markey, Enid, 28
Marmont, Percy, 39
Marriage Cheat, The, 39
Marriage Italian Style, 317
Married Flirts, 93
Marsh, Mae, 29, 273
Marshall, Alan, 213
Marshall, Herbert, 107, 237
Martin, Mary, 115
Marx, Groucho, 218
Marx, Harpo, 219
Masina, Giulietta, 290
Mason, James, 284
Mason, LeRoy, 56
Massey, Raymond, 127
Mastroianni, Marcello, 317
Mature, Victor, 273
Mayerling, 337
Mayo, Virginia, 230
McCabe and Mrs. Miller, 322
McCrea, Joel, 163
McDaniel, Hattie, 174
McDowall, Roddy, 234
McDowell, Claire, 63
McGregor, Malcolm, 36
McGuire, Dorothy, 245
McQueen, Butterfly, 174
Meighan, Thomas, 28
Member of the Wedding, The, 265
Menjou, Adolphe, 150

Mercouri, Melina, 322
Merry Widow, The, 266
Midsummer Night's Dream, A, 178
Mighty Barnum, The, 150
Miles, Sarah, 318
Milky Way, The, 135
Milland, Ray, 147
Mills, John, 205
Minter, Mary Miles, 31
Miranda, Carmen, 218
Miranda, Isa, 177
Misfits, The, 348
Miss Sadie Thompson, 271
Mr. Robinson Crusoe, 111
Mr. Skeffington, 242
Mrs. Miniver, 235
Mitchell, Thomas, 174, 188
Mitchum, Robert, 220
Moby Dick, 262
Modern Times, 95
Mogambo, 263
Mohr, Hal, 108
Monks, Jimmy, 227
Monroe, Marilyn, 260, 261, 308, 348
Monsieur Vincent, 210
Montand, Yves, 365
Montgomery, Douglass, 140
Moonshine and Honeysuckle, 31
Moore, Colleen, 68
Moore, Dickie, 166
Moore, Matt, 153
Moorehead, Agnes, 200
Moreau, Jeanne, 335, 347
Morgan, Ralph, 150
Moulin Rouge, 278
Mourning Becomes Electra, 192
Muni, Paul, 134
Murder Most Foul, 327
*Murderers are Amongst Us, The
(Die Morder sind Unter Uns),* 208
Murray, Mae, 60
Murray, Tom, 95
Music in the Air, 132
Myers, Carmel, 62
My Fair Lady, 367
My Man, 102
Mysterious Dr. Fu Manchu, 171
Napoleon, 53
Navigator, The, 48
Nazimova, Alla, 54, 97
Neagle, Anna, 172, 232
Negri, Pola, 61, 108
Newman, Paul, 256, 319
Nicholson, Jack, 338
Night Heaven Fell, The, 289
Night in Casablanca, A, 219
Night of Love, The, 66
Nilsson, Anna Q., 35
Normand, Mabel, 34

Novak, Kim, 255, 300, 301
Novarro, Ramon, 43, 63, 136
Nun's Story, The, 283
Oberon, Merle, 122, 213
Objective Burma, 228
O'Brien, George, 76, 77
Of Human Bondage, 141
O'Hara, Maureen, 217
Oklahoma, 288
Oland, Warner, 171
Old Man and the Sea, The, 268
Oliver, 323
Olivier, Laurence, 122, 197, 334
O'Neal, Jennifer, 353
O'Neal, Tatum, 338
One Million Years B.C., 310
*One Woman's Story (The Passionate
Friends),* 227
On the Beach, 258
On the Waterfront, 275
Orphans of the Storm, 40
Orpheus (Orphée), 286
O'Toole, Peter, 321, 330
Outlaw, The, 216
Outrage, The, 331
Page, Geraldine, 345
Paid, 140
Palance, Jack, 274
Palmer, Lilli, 128
Paluzzi, Lucianna, 314
Paper Moon, 338
Pardon Us, 112
Parker, Jean, 108
Parker, Suzy, 307
*Passion of Joan of Arc, The
(La Passion de Jeanne d'Arc),* 57
Paxinou, Katina, 233
Peck, Gregory, 190, 203, 288
Perfect Understanding, 139
Perkins, Anthony, 350
Perkins, Millie, 265
Perrin, Jacques, 317
Personal Property, 177
Peter Ibbetson, 107
Petroff, Boris, 142
Phantom, The, 28
Phantom of the Opera, The, 41
Philbin, Mary, 41
Philipe, Gerard, 287
Pickford, Mary, 31, 78, 153
Pidgeon, Walter, 234
Pink Panther, The, 326
Place in the Sun, A, 280
Pleasure Buyers, The, 72
Plummer, Christopher, 355
Poitier, Sidney, 270
Porgy and Bess, 270
Potter, Martin, 328
Powell, Eleanor, 158

Powell, William, 90
Power, Tyrone, 255
Preston, Robert, 240
Price, Vincent, 131
Pringle, Aileen, 83
Prisoner of Zenda, The, 93
Private Life of Henry VIII, The, 127
*Private Lives of Elizabeth and Essex,
The,* 131
Promise at Dawn, 322
Pumpkin Eater, The, 351
Pursuit of Happiness, The, 116
Quai des Brumes, 140
Queen Christina, 120, 121
Queen Elizabeth, 17
Queen Kelly, 83
Quinn, Anthony, 291
Raft, George, 208
Rag Man, The, 59
Rainer, Luise, 164
Rains, Claude, 160, 242
Rasputin and the Empress, 150, 173
Rasumny, Mikhail, 233
Rathbone, Basil, 168
Ray, Aldo, 271
Raye, Martha, 115
Raymond, Gene, 153
Red Dust, 144
Redford, Robert, 315
Redgrave, Vanessa, 329
Reed, Carol, 323
Remick, Lee, 281
Rennie, James, 74
Resurrection, 109
Revenge, 56
Revere, Anne, 203
Rice, John C., 8
Rich, Irene, 72
Rich, Lillian, 73
Rico, Mona, 87
Riva, Emmanuelle, 262
Road to Zanzibar, 217
Robe, The, 272, 272
Roberts, Rachel, 342
Robinson, Edward G., 156
Rogers, Charles "Buddy," 69, 70
Rogers, Ginger, 118, 176
Roland, Gilbert, 73, 89
Roman, Ruth, 267
Roman Spring of Mrs. Stone, The, 347
Romeo and Juliet, 171, 273
Rosemary's Baby, 340
Rose of the Golden West, 89
Ross, Diana, 314
Ross, Katharine, 341
Royal Hunt of the Sun, The, 355
Ruman, Sig, 219
Russell, Jane, 216
Russell, Rosalind, 192

Rutherford, Ann, 174
Rutherford, Margaret, 204, 327
Ryan's Daughter, 318
Sahara, 229
Saint, Eva Marie, 275
Salter, Thelma, 36
Sanda, Dominique, 318
Sanders, George, 220
Say One For Me, 278
Scarlet Pimpernel, The, 127
Schell, Maria, 256
Scott, George C., 311
Scott, Randolph, 231
Sea Hawk, The, 130
Sears, Laura, 36
Seberg, Jean, 299
Secret Agent, 154
Secret of Santa Vittoria, 316, 364
Sellers, Peter, 326
Separate Tables, 296
Seventh Heaven, 86
Seventh Seal, The, 277
Shall We Dance, 176
Sharif, Omar, 337
Shearer, Norma, 161
Shentall, Susan, 273
Sheridan, Ann, 194
Shigeta, James, 262
Ship of Fools, 350
Sidney, Basil, 197
Sidney, Sylvia, 124
Sign of the Cross, The, 133
Signoret, Simone, 350
Simmons, Jean, 204, 279
Simon, Michel, 353
Simpson, Russell, 191
Single Standard, The, 65
Sin of Madelon Claudet, The, 124
Sins of Her Parent, 37
Six Days, 33
Skippy, 167
Skipworth, Alison, 113
Slumberland, 36
Smilin' Through, 161
Smith, Alexis, 207
Sokoloff, Vladimir, 233
So Long Letty, 123
Somebody Up There Likes Me, 256
Song of Scheherazade, 195
Son of the Sheik, 45
Sons and Lovers, 342
Spiral Staircase, The, 245
Stack, Robert, 187
Stage Fright, 296

Staiola, Enzo, 243
Stanwyck, Barbara, 148, 164, 199, 237, 368
Star, 357
Steiger, Rod, 312
Stein, Paul L., 108
Stella Dallas, 148
Sten, Anna, 109
Stewart, James, 158
Stockwell, Dean, 213
Story of Temple Drake, The, 149
Street Angel, 84
Streetcar Named Desire, A, 294, 295
Streisand, Barbra, 336
Sullivan's Travels, 234
Summer and Smoke, 345
Summer of '42, 353
Sun Also Rises, The, 303
Sunrise, 76, 77
Sunset Boulevard, 246
Suspicion, 215
Swanson, Gloria, 49, 83, 99, 132, 139, 246
Sweet Charity, 324
Talmadge, Constance, 91
Talmadge, Norma, 73
Taming of the Shrew, The, 78
Tarzan Escapes, 111
Taylor, Elizabeth, 249, 280, 360, 361
Taylor, Robert, 177
Tellegen, Lou,
Temple, Shirley, 167
Terry, Alice, 93
Test of Honor, The, 24
That Hamilton Woman, 236, 241
They Shoot Horses, Don't They?, 339
This Sporting Life, 342
Three Violent People, 292
Thunderball, 314
Tierney, Gene, 187
Todd, Ann, 227
Todd, Richard, 296
Tom Jones, 356
Tone, Franchot, 188
Topper Returns, 248
Torres, Raquel, 136
Tracy, Spencer, 268
Treasure of Sierra Madre, The, 231
Trojan Women, The, 354
True Grit, 333
Tryon, Tom, 292
Tugboat Annie, 112
Tulsa, 240
Turner, Lana, 192, 221, 252, 266

Twelvetrees, Helen, 104, 117
Twiggy, 328
Two-Faced Woman, 198
Two of Us, The, 353
Unholy Three, The, 96
Ure, Mary, 342
Valentino, Rudolph, 44, 45
Van Rooten, Luis, 285
Veidt, Conrad, 35
Velez, Lupe, 79, 159
Victoria the Great, 172
Viva Maria, 335
Von Stroheim, Erich, 51
Wager, Anthony, 204
Wagner, Robert, 278
Walking Hills, The, 231
Waters, Ethel, 265
Wayne, John, 333
Wedding March, The, 50, 51
Welch, Raquel, 310
Welles, Orson, 214
Weissmuller, Johnny, 111
Werner, Oskar, 350
West, Mae, 142
West Side Story, 325
Wharf Rat, The, 29
When Tomorrow Comes, 156
Whisperers, The, 343
White, Alice, 81
White Cargo, 207
Whittier, Robert, 53
Widmark, Richard, 213
Wild River, 281
Wild Strawberries, 276
Wings, 69
Winters, Shelley, 274
Without Limit, 35
Witness for the Prosecution, 257
Wizard of Oz, The, 179
Woman Commands, A, 104
Woman of Experience, A, 104
Wong, Anna May, 165
Wood, Natalie, 281
Woodward, Joanne, 293
World, Flesh and the Devil, The, 292
Wray, Fay, 50
Wrong Man, The, 274
Wuthering Heights, 122
Wynyard, Diana, 173
York, Michael, 352
York, Susannah, 356
Young, Loretta, 168
Young, Robert, 123

Acknowledgments

I am grateful to the following for their assistance in the preparation of this book: Academy of Motion Picture Arts and Sciences; Irving Adler, Paramount Pictures; John E. Allen, Inc.; Marie Baxter, *Look* Magazine; Ralph Buck, United Artists; James Card, George Eastman House; William K. Everson; Monroe Friedman, Universal Pictures; Herb Honis, United Artists; Norman Kaphan, Metro-Goldwyn-Mayer; Jack Kerness, Columbia Pictures; Jack Lyons, Paramount Pictures; Lou Marino, Warner Brothers; Museum of Modern Art; George C. Pratt, George Eastman House; Mark Ricci; Jonas Rosenfield, Jr., Twentieth Century-Fox; Ella Smith; Charles L. Turner; Lou Valentino; Douglas Whitney; Leo Wilder, Warner Brothers.

R.L. 1973